The PORTAL

GOD'S DOORWAY TO HEAVEN

BILL HOWARD

Charleston, AR

COBB PUBLISHING

2023

Published in the United States of America by:

Cobb Publishing
704 E. Main St.
Charleston, AR 72993
Editor@CobbPublishing.com
www.CobbPublishing.com
479.747.8372

Cover artwork by Paul Cobb (PaulLoganCobb@gmail.com)
Interior layout and editing by Bradley S. Cobb

All Scripture from KJV unless otherwise noted.
ISBN: 978-1-960858-39-9

Dedication

Giving thought as to where to begin with the dedication of this or any of the other writings by this author, the first thing that comes to mind is that my wife Juanita should be listed as co-author. From the first book to this, she has been the source of encouragement to keep me going. She works diligently in editing and keeping my mistakes to a minimum, and without her encouragement and commitment to my work, there likely would be less of it.

To those who have read my books and given me encouragement, I thank each of you. It is my hope that those who read this book will be enlightened and spiritually strengthened. There can be no subject of greater impact on our lives than the love and mercy of God and His will for all people of the world.

Chapter One

"To everything thing there is a season, and a time to every purpose under the heaven" (Ecclesiastes 3:1). This fact is so because God deemed it to be that way. Let's go back a bit and give some consideration to what we will term "prehistory" for lack of a better title. The beginning words of written history go like this: "In beginning God created the heaven and the earth" (Genesis 1:1). Everything before this time is prehistory and that is where we find the one true and living God: in eternity, the era before recorded history when eternity was the only realm of existence and was the habitation of our God. This period antedates the dawn of history. While we may not fully comprehend, we must accept that God exists, has always existed in this realm we call eternity, and is a Sovereign being, though a spirit, yet a supreme being with extreme intelligence and unlimited power. The power to say, "let there be" and it comes to pass.

Eternity can be best described as that which has always been and will always be; it is a place that is timeless. There was no beginning and will be no end so time is of no consideration there; just as God is timeless, has always been and will always be. It was from this prehistorical place that God was making His plans for an event that is beyond the capability of mortal man to fully comprehend. It will forever be recognized as the most magnificent, most glorious and marvelous occurrence ever. Prior to this event, there was only God, Christ, and the Holy Spirit, and we have no idea how long God was deliberating and finalizing His plans for this happening. What we do know is that before He began to unfold His plan, there was no earth, no Universe, no people. We are told "the earth was without form and void; and darkness was on the face of the deep" (Genesis 1:2).

When God had completed His plan, which was all-encompassing and would be valid from that point until mankind is facing the final segment of eternity, He began the creation of all that exists in the world today: the elegant and majestic Universe, the Heavens, the Earth and all the components of each. An undertaking far beyond the capability of man to be able to fully grasp. The first command was: "Let there be light," and there was light; and the creation continued for a full six days; and when He was finished, He rested on the seventh day. So, in six days, God had completed the creation and made available for all the world that was to come a plethora of opportunities for mankind in which he would have the means and the opportunity to attain a beautiful relationship with the Almighty God.

God threw open the door of eternity, He created the Portal through which mankind can seek and find the course of action that will lead to living forever in the presence of God. "He hath made the earth by His power, He hath established the world by His wisdom, and hath stretched out the heavens by His discretion" (Jeremiah 10:12). For something to be brought into being, to begin to take place, there must of necessity be a first cause. Everything obviously must begin with something. God is that first cause; He is the cause and has the omnipotence to create. "Thou, even thou, art Lord alone; thou hast made heaven, the heaven of heavens, with all their host, the earth, and all things that are therein, the seas, and all that is therein, and thou preservest them all"

(Nehemiah 9:6). God spoke, and it came into existence, He commanded, and it was established. "By the word of the Lord were the heavens made; and all the host of them by the breath of His mouth" (Psalm 33:6). "Through faith we understand that the worlds were framed by the word of God, so that things which are seen were not made of things which do appear" (Hebrews 11:3).

The four truths we discovered so far is that (1) eternity exists, (2) God was forever dwelling in that place, (3) God is the creator of all that exists, and (4) He has a perpetual plan for all of mankind that was completed before creation. "In hope of eternal life, which God, that cannot lie, PROMISED BEFORE THE WORLD BEGAN" (Titus 1:2). "Who (God) hath saved us, and called us with an holy calling, not according to our works, but according to His own purpose and grace, which was given us in Christ Jesus BEFORE THE WORLD BEGAN" (2 Timothy 1:9). God is the one who saved us from the punishment of sin, not because of anything we have done, but because of His love He chose mankind to be saved from the beginning. These truths from God's word remove any doubt about God's plan being complete before He began the creation.

Chapter Two

We have taken our scriptures from the book of beginnings, the book of NEW: Genesis. With this information, we begin with nothing other than God, and we progress to the creation, then to the beginning of God's unveiling of His master plan which will be the guiding beacon for every event that will transpire from creation to the final judgment of mankind and beyond, infinite eternity. "In the beginning was the Word, and the Word was with God, and the Word was God. The same was in the beginning with God. All things were made by Him; and without Him was not any thing made that was made" (John 1:1-3). "And the Word was made flesh, and dwelt among us, (and we beheld His glory, the glory as of the only begotten of the Father,) full of grace and truth" (John 1:14). The psalmist said: "By the word of the Lord were the heavens made; their starry host of them by the breath of His mouth" (Psalm 33:6). In the words of Moses: "O Lord God, thou hast begun to show thy servant thy greatness, and thy mighty hand: for what God is there in heaven or in earth, that can do according to thy works, and according to thy might?" (Deuteronomy 3:24). God said: "I have made the earth, the man and the beast that are upon the ground, by my great power and by my outstretched arm, and have given it unto whom it seemed meet unto me" (Jeremiah 27:5). And again: "Ah Lord God! Behold thou hast made the heaven and the earth by thy great power and stretched out arm, and there is nothing too hard for thee" (Jeremiah 32:17).

Considering creation, it is difficult to perceive the reality of such an event taking place—and then to assimilate it in our understanding is a difficult process. However, if one will gaze into the heavens above on a clear night and perceive the blazing glory of that heavenly body, the dazzling beauty and magnificence we see, it will remove any doubt about the power of the Almighty God. Abraham Lincoln once made the statement: "I can see how it might be possible for a man to look down on the earth and be an atheist, but I cannot conceive how he could look up into the heavens and say there is no God." What an astute observation by Lincoln and one with which each of us can agree. We will go back to the book of NEW.

"Thus the heavens and the earth were finished, and all the host of them" (Genesis 2:1). With the creation of man on the sixth day, God had completed His work: "And God saw everything He had made, and behold it was very good" (Genesis 1:31), and was satisfied and rested on the seventh day: "And on the seventh day God ended His work which He had made" (Genesis 2:2b). Now let's consider this: the creation of man was the culmination of God finishing His work of the six days. "And God said, 'Let us make man in our image, after our likeness: and let them have dominion over the fish of the sea, and over the fowl of the air, and over the cattle, and over all the earth, and over every creeping thing that creepeth upon the earth.' So God created man in his own image, in the image of God created He him; male and female created He them" (Genesis 1:26-27). "And the Lord God formed man of the dust of the ground and breathed into his nostrils the breath of life; and man became a living soul" (Genesis 2:7).

God's plan was being executed just as He intended. Something else came into play; man now existed and that required God to make an abode for man. This was about four thousand years before the birth of Jesus Christ. "And the Lord God planted a garden eastward in Eden; and there He put man whom He had formed" (Genesis 2:8). As the garden was being formed, God planted every tree that is pleasant to the sight and good for food: the tree of life also in the midst of the garden and the tree of knowledge of good and evil. (Genesis 2:9). We'll go back again for a little more information about man.

Is it possible that we can visualize what we have been reading? Quite difficult, isn't it? God has created what we believe to be the most beautiful abode with every need of man fulfilled. All man must do is take care of it, eat of everything in the garden with one exception. God provided for him a helper, a woman to be his wife. He had dominion over everything that God had made; his responsibility was to dress and keep the garden, be fruitful and multiply, replenish the earth and subdue it. And God said to Adam, the man: "of every tree of the garden thou mayest freely eat but of the tree of the knowledge of good and evil, thou shalt not eat of it: for in the day that thou eatest thereof thou shalt surely die" (2:16-17). He had a cinch, everything imaginable that one could need was furnished in the most beautiful place in God's creation. How could it be any better than this? Not a lot to do, plenty to eat, a wife to share the work and be his mate. What a happy ending to a splendid story. But wait, the story did not end at that point. Something took place that should have never happened. Evidently there was a breakdown in communication or a misunderstanding and another major event is in the offing. God is unhappy and that is never a good thing. Let's pursue this and see what we can determine.

It is evident that something had gone awry. Was there a hiccup in God's plan? No, that could not happen, the plan is perfect; so, what is the problem? There was a dereliction in man's conduct. God had given instruction about eating the fruit of the tree of the knowledge of good and evil; they were not to touch it. This was a divine commandment. If they ate the fruit of that tree, they would surely die. That was simple and direct: disobey and pay the price.

Chapter Three

"Now the serpent (Satan) was more subtle than any beast of the field which the Lord God had made. And he said unto the woman, 'Yea hath God said, ye shall not eat of every tree of the garden?' And the woman said unto the serpent, 'we may eat of the fruit of the trees of the garden: but of the fruit of the tree which is in the midst of the garden, God hath said, ye shall not eat of it, neither shall ye touch it, lest ye die'" (Genesis 3:1-3). So, here is the hitch, the serpent lied to Eve. He said: "For God doth know that in the day ye eat thereof, then your eyes shall be opened, and ye shall be as gods, knowing good and evil" (Genesis 3:5). Eve was tempted and succumbed to that temptation; she did what she was instructed not to do. It was a terrible mistake on her part. Satan deceived her with a lie, and she, knowing what the penalty would be, deliberately disobeyed God and ate the fruit of that tree. She added to her sin by tempting Adam, and he wasn't any smarter than she was; he also ate the fruit.

God had blessed them with a perfect home where their every need would be fulfilled, and they foolishly disobeyed Him. In doing so, they brought sin and death into the world. The Apostle Paul would later write: "Wherefore, as by one man sin entered into the world, and death by sin; and so, death passed upon all men, for that all have sinned" (Romans 5:12). This was not something which God wanted for mankind. He knew it would happen, but it was not His desire. Because of the sin they committed, He would punish them. They were cast from the garden, lost their grand home, and their life would be changed drastically. To Eve:

"I will greatly multiply thy sorrow and thy conception; in sorrow thou shalt bring forth children" (Genesis 3:16a), needless suffering that has passed to women through the ages. To Adam: "Cursed is the ground for thy sake; in sorrow shalt thou eat of it all the days of thy life; Thorns and thistles shall it bring forth to thee; and thou shall eat the herb of the field; In the sweat of thy face shalt thou eat bread" (Genesis 17b-19a). A far cry from the garden from which they had been ejected. The most tragic aspect of the situation is that they not only lost their home, but they lost the personal contact with God. He would no longer walk and talk with them as He did in the garden. Sin had separated them from their creator, their God.

With those troubles behind them, Adam and Eve went to work fulfilling requirements that God had placed on them. They began to multiply and populate the earth, and everything would settle in and be normal, and God would bless them in those ways they needed.

However, it didn't really work out that way for too many years. We cannot pinpoint exactly how many years had passed, but about fifteen hundred at least when man again aggravated God. "And God saw that the wickedness of man was great in the earth, and that every imagination of the thoughts of his heart was only evil continually. And it repented the Lord that He had made man on the earth, and it grieved Him at His heart" (Genesis 6:5-6). Perhaps our first thought might be: "Oh no, not again!" It wasn't too long ago that God was disappointed in His creation for their disobedience and punished them severely; what is taking place now? The world is corrupt and filled with violence, so God regretted that He had created man. The wanton wickedness

13

and gross immorality that was prevalent sickened God. He was tired of dealing with people who were so abominable in His sight; He wanted nothing more to do with them. They would all be wiped off the face of the earth. The Bible tells us that one man found grace in the sight of the Lord. Noah and his family were to be spared. It is a favorite story which has been covered many times. Refresh your memory and read again Genesis chapters six through nine. Noah was given specific instructions for building an ark and spent one hundred twenty years building and telling others of the coming destruction—God was going to destroy the earth. In the end, only Noah, his wife and three sons and their wives were saved in the ark, plus representatives of all the wildlife, as God had instructed.

What is the most outstanding consideration in our thoughts so far? It is how thankless man has been to the God who created him and has blessed him with every need and requirement, yet man continues to turn his back on God and has been disobedient to all that God has asked.

It was only a few hundred years later that God was again disheartened by the actions of those He created. There was much wickedness and corruption in Sodom and Gomorrah and God would again be inclined to destroy. "And the Lord said, because the cry of Sodom and Gomorrah is great, and because their sin is very grievous; I will go down now and see whether they have done altogether according to the cry of it, which is come unto me; and if not, I will know" (Genesis 18:20-21). Abraham was concerned and questioned the Lord. "Peradventure there be fifty righteous within the city: wilt thou also destroy and not spare the place for the fifty righteous that are therein?" (Genesis 18:24). He continued to badger God and in the end, God agreed to save them if only ten could be found; God agreed to this. It was a pitiful situation but not even ten could be found, and God rained fire and brimstone on the cities, and they were utterly destroyed. Lot, his wife, and two daughters escaped. They were instructed not to look back as they departed the city, but Lot's wife disobeyed, and as she turned to look, she was turned into a pilar of salt. Another instance of tragedy for not doing as God has directed, another case of disobeying and paying the price.

Chapter Four

Beginning with the Patriarchal age, from the beginning of man until the time when Moses was given the Law on Mt. Sinai, which was about fifteen hundred years before the coming of the Messiah, the fathers were the leaders of the families and the tribes. They were responsible for the obedience of their clan in respect to God's wishes and the worship of those in the group. They were recognized as an absolute authority and were accountable to God for the actions of their family. Despite all the blessings that were imparted to them, the Hebrews seemed to have a proclivity to be hardheaded, stiff-necked and determined to ignore God's wishes far too often. It didn't end there either; it was their way of directing their activities until the destruction of Jerusalem in AD 70. More on this later.

The writer of the Hebrew letter wrote that at different times and in several ways, God spoke to the fathers by the prophets, Hebrews 1:1. That indicates that whatever needed to be known or acted upon, God was the one who advised the leaders. So often we think of the patriarchal period as dealing primarily with Abraham, Isaac, and Jacob, and though they were patriarchs, so were many others. While Abraham is Israel's ancestor, Moses is often thought of as its founder. He was a Prophet of God as we find in the book of Deuteronomy. "And there arose not a Prophet since in Israel like unto Moses, whom the Lord knew face to face" (Deuteronomy 34:10). A Prophet was one who was sent out to speak for another, so Moses was a leader and a Prophet until the time he released his responsibilities to Joshua. He spoke for God to the people in early times. He spoke to Pharoah for God; he spoke to the Israelites as he brought them out of Egypt and for forty years of wandering in the wilderness.

Israel was considered the "seed of Abraham" because of the covenant that God made with Abraham. After the death of Terah, Abrams father, the Lord spoke to Abram: "Get thee out of thy country, and from thy kindred, and from thy father's house, unto a land I will show thee; And I will make of thee a great nation, and I will bless thee, and make thy name great; and thou shalt be a blessing: And I will bless them that bless thee, and curse him that curseth thee: and in thee shall all families of the earth be blessed" (Genesis 12:1-3). Abram obeyed God and departed from Haran at the age of seventy-five. Through the years this entailed several moves and finally winding up in Egypt because of a famine in the area of Bethel. Because of their lying to Pharaoh, he was plagued, and sent them out of Egypt with all their holdings, which was a great amount of wealth. Abram's name was later changed to Abraham, and he, Isaac, and Jacob were the primary leaders in the patriarchal age.

Chapter Five

Reading in the book of Judges we find that after the death of Joshua, disorganization was widespread and there was tribal discord. The people cried unto the Lord and He raised up Judges who saved them. "Nevertheless the Lord raised up judges, which delivered them out of the hand of those who spoiled them" (Judges 2:16). "And when the Lord raised them up judges, then the Lord was with the judge, and delivered them out of the hand of their enemies all the days of the judge: for it repented the Lord because of their groanings by reason of them that oppressed them and vexed them" (Judges 2:18). "Judges and officers shalt thou make thee in all thy gates, which the Lord thy God giveth thee, throughout thy tribes: and they shall judge the people with just judgment" (Deuteronomy 16:18).

Because of the growth of the Israelites, Moses was overburdened dealing with the needs of the people. Jethro advised him to appoint judges who could hear the cases and make a judgment call. For the weightier matters, Moses told them to bring them to him. "So Moses hearkened to the voice of his father in law, and did all that he had said. And Moses chose able men out of all Israel, and made them heads over the people, rulers of thousands, rulers of hundreds, rulers of fifties, and rulers of tens. And they judged the people at all seasons: the hard causes they brought unto Moses, but every small matter they judged themselves" (Exodus 18:24-26). We are not privy to the exact number of years the judges administered over Israel, but it ranges between three hundred fifty and four hundred ten years, and it lasted until the appointment of Saul as the first King. There is at times a bit of disagreement about the number of judges, but the text indicates that there were fourteen: Othneil was the first and Samuel was the last.

There is a unique meaning to the term "able" in Moses choosing. Those chosen for the position would be above reproach; this is an honored calling. They were to work with Moses in the guiding of the people, adhering to the laws of the land and to comprehend what is best for all concerned. To do God's will on earth as it would be done in heaven because all human authority comes from God. If you wish to know more about this, an excellent reading on the subject will be found in Deuteronomy 1:9-18.

"And it came to pass, when Samuel was old, that he made his sons judges over Israel" (1 Samuel 8:1). The Bible tells us that Joel and Abiah walked not in the ways of Samuel. They turned aside after money, took bribes and were not just. "Then all the Elders of Israel gathered themselves together, and came to Samuel unto Ramah, and said unto him, behold, thou art old, and thy sons walk not in thy ways: now make us a king to judge us like all the nations" (1 Samuel 8:4-5). Samuel was not happy about this, but the Lord counseled him. Go ahead and give them what they want, they have not rejected you, they have rejected me. "According to all the works which they have done since the day that I brought them up out of Egypt even unto this day, wherewith they have forsaken me, and served other gods, so do they also unto thee. Now therefore hearken unto their voice" (1 Samuel 8:8-9a). Samuel told them the hardships they would endure with kings over them, but they insisted all the more.

"Nevertheless, the people refused to obey the voice of Samuel: and they said, nay; but we will have a king over us; that we also may be like all the nations; and that our king may judge us, and go out before us, and fight our battles" (1 Samuel 8:19-20). So, the Lord told Samuel to make them a king. Typical of the Jews, it seems nothing could satisfy them for too long a period of time. Moses had a great need of men to help him with caring for the people, thus the advent of the Judges, and this was satisfactory for a while, but eventually the Israelites were unhappy with this and demanded to have a king so they would be like other nations.

Even with the warning of Samuel about the problems and hardships they would endure with a king, they insisted that their choice was to have a king, so it was granted to them.

Chapter Six

About 1095 to 1050 BCE, Israel's wishes were acknowl-
edged, and the first king over Israel was anointed. "Now the
Lord had told Samuel in his ear a day before Saul came,
saying, Tomorrow about this time I will send thee a man out
of the land of Benjamin, and thou shalt anoint him to be cap-
tain over my people Israel, that he may save my people out
of the hand of the Philistines: for I have looked upon my
people, because their cry is unto me. And when Samuel saw
Saul, the Lord said unto him, Behold the man whom I spake
to thee of! This same shall reign over my people" (1 Samuel
9:15-17). So, Saul the son of Kish and grandson of Abiel
was set apart by the lord to be the first king over Israel. We
will not dwell too much on the kings, but 1 Samuel chapters
nine through thirty-one depict pretty much the story of Saul.
According to history, Saul was muscular and tall with a
great physique, and was kingly to his friends and generous
to his foes. He was a man of valor in battle and was not harsh
with the defeated. Unfortunately, Saul was a disappointment
and neglected his responsibilities. Samuel rebuked him
three times for his failures and severed ties with Saul. Saul
reigned for 37 years and was followed by David who
reigned for 40 years (seven years over Judah, and 33 years
over all of Israel), and then Solomon who reigned for 40
years. These were followed by twenty-one others, covering
a period of a bit over five hundred years—Zedekiah being
the last.

It was not on the agenda to cover in depth the period of the judges and kings of Israel. To accomplish that would require several books and many years. What we have covered is a brief summary of circumstances which are pertinent to our study.

The failures of the Jews to heed God's wishes for them is evident throughout the entire Old Testament. We have not considered all of their transgressions, but enough to show how inconsistent they were in their dealing with the God who was the source of their every blessing. As we continue our study of the Israelites, we witness the continuing disobedience and the habitual turning away from God's decrees.

At one time Moses chastened them because of their rebelliousness. "And at Taberah, and at Massah, and at Kibroth-hattavah, ye provoked the Lord to wrath. Likewise when the Lord sent you from Kadesh-barnea, saying, Go up and possess the land which I have given you; then ye rebelled against the commandment of the Lord your God, and ye believed Him not, nor harkened to His voice. Ye have been rebellious against the Lord from the day that I knew you" (Deuteronomy 9:22-24). It was at this time Moses prayed for forty days and forty nights to God that He would not destroy them. This is just one of the occasions this happened; there were many other times they made God very unhappy with them.

We could think a bit about their actions when God sent Moses to lead them out of bondage to the Egyptians. They began the journey complaining and did so most of the time. They complained at the Red Sea because the Egyptians were pursuing them. They defied God when Moses was on the mountain receiving the commandments. They talked Aaron into making a golden idol, saying this is the god that would lead them. Despite this attitude, God provided water, food and guidance for them. On a trip that should have taken maybe twelve days, they wandered in the wilderness for forty years because of their rebellious spirit and disobedience. Even then, God did not allow their garments or their shoes or sandals to wear out during that long time.

What we have considered to this point is a summation of the lack of adherence to God's wishes, the continuation of sin that began in the Garden of Eden. We realize that sin has created the chasm between man and the God of creation, the God of all blessings, and this is not what He wishes. As previously stated, God's plan was perfect, but man was not. This vast separation between God and man must of necessity be overcome, and a way for man to be reconciled to God provided. So, His plan continues to be unveiled according to His strategy decided upon before creation.

With this much history under our belt, we would be remiss if we did not pursue further knowledge of what God's future plans must be. A good portion of what we have considered up to this point has been slanted on the negative side: unruly, disobedient people, complaining and going against God's wishes. God's plan must contain the means of overcoming the man's mistakes of the past and bringing the people back into a proper relationship with Him. So, lets dig for more facts that are in keeping with accomplishing the overall plan designed for the good of mankind.

Chapter Seven

As we noted earlier in the writing, a prophet is one that is sent out to speak for another. In the Old Testament, prophets were very important individuals. They were appointed by God to disseminate what God had chosen to disclose to the people. They were able to do this because the Holy Spirit was their guide. In view of circumstances to this point, it was time for more of God's intentions to be known.

There were many prophets in the Old Testament, and Isaiah was one of the predominate ones. He was a contemporary of Micah, another prophet. Isaiah was not the first to speak of a coming Messiah, but these are his words in the text: "Therefore the Lord Himself shall give you a sign; Behold, a virgin shall conceive, and bear a son, and shall call his name Immanuel" (Isaiah 7:14). This prophecy would certainly create questions. He was saying something was going to happen that could not possibly happen: "a virgin would conceive and bear a son." That is not in keeping with natural events in human beings. However, when Matthew was writing his gospel, he referred to that scripture. "Behold, a virgin shall be with child, and shall bring forth a son, and they shall call his name Emmanuel, which being interpreted is, God with us" (Matthew 1:23). So, we are being made privy to a fascinating predicted event. We will certainly need to know more about this, so we will pursue the story further.

Again, the words of the prophet: "For unto us a child is born, unto us a son is given: and the government shall be upon his shoulder: and his name shall be called Wonderful,

Counsellor, The mighty God, The everlasting Father, The Prince of Peace" (Isaiah 9:6). From the gospel of Luke, we learn more. "And in the sixth month the angel Gabriel was sent from God unto a city of Galilee, named Nazareth, to a virgin espoused to a man whose name was Joseph, of the house of David; and the virgin's name was Mary. And the angel came in unto her, and said, Hail, thou art highly favored, the Lord is with thee: blessed art thou among women. And the angel said unto her, fear not, Mary: for thou hast found favor with God. And, behold, thou shalt conceive in thy womb, and bring forth a son, and shalt call his name Jesus" (Luke 1:26-28 and 30-31). "Then Mary said unto the angel, "How shall this be, seeing I know not a man?" "And the angel answered and said unto her, the Holy Spirit shall come upon thee, and the power of the highest shall overshadow thee: therefore also that holy thing which shall be born of thee shall be called the Son of God" (Luke 1:34-35). The angel of the Lord told Joseph: "thou son of David, fear not to take unto thee Mary thy wife: for that which is conceived in her is of the Holy Spirit. And she shall bring forth a son, and thou shalt call his name Jesus: for He shall save his people from their sins" (Matthew 1:20-21). More of God's agenda is being revealed; this is what He intended before there was reckoning of time. By this miracle, a virgin, having never been with a man, is pregnant. The angel Gabriel told Mary and Joseph that this miracle of a virgin conceiving was of God.

Perhaps some of these things are difficult for us to comprehend. However, we do not have to know everything that God has in his plans. Moses said: "the secret things belong unto the Lord our God: but those things which are revealed belong to us and to our children forever, that we may do all the words of this law" (Deuteronomy 29:29).

God gives us the information that he chooses for us to have, and He reveals these things to us in a timely fashion. Up to this point, we have learned of God's love for man, we have witnessed the creation of all that exists, we have seen the great blessings that God has bestowed upon mankind. However, what we also have witnessed is the fact that man has consistently disobeyed God, and oftentimes turned his back upon God and deliberately done things, knowing God did not approve.

As we pointed out earlier, man brought sin into the world, and sin is what separates man from God. Elijah said: "I have been very jealous for the Lord God of hosts: for the children of Israel have forsaken thy covenant, thrown down thine altars, and slain thy prophets with the sword; and I, even I only, am left; and they seek my life to take it away" (1 Kings 19:10). Also, "nevertheless they were disobedient, and rebelled against thee, and cast thy law behind their backs, and slew thy prophets which testified against them to turn them to thee, and they wrought great provocations. Therefore thou deliveredst them into the hand of their enemies, who vexed them: and in the time of their trouble, when they cried unto thee, thou heardest them from heaven; and according to thy manifold mercies thou gavest them saviors, who saved them out of the hand of their enemies, but after they had rest, they did evil again before thee: therefore leftest thou them in the hand of their enemies, so that they had dominion over them: yet when they returned, and cried unto thee, thou heardest them from heaven; and many times didst thou deliver them according to thy mercies" (Nehemiah

9:26-28). This was typical of the activities of the Israelites, disobeying time and time again.

In view of their behavior, we wonder about God's mercy and his love for the creature which He created and why He is so forgiving. Yet, He chose to make a way for men to be able to be reconciled to him and not lose the blessings which He has in store for mankind on earth, and the ultimate blessing of being with Him in eternity.

Now, we can come to a full understanding of the meaning in John 3:16-17. "For God so loved the world, that He gave His only begotten Son, that whosoever believeth in him should not perish, but have everlasting life. For God sent not his Son into the world to condemn the world but that the world through him might be saved." Also, the apostle John stated: "In this was manifested the love of God toward us, because that God sent his only begotten son into the world that we might live through him. Herein is love, not that we loved God, but that He loved us and sent His Son to be the propitiation for our sins" (1 John 4:9-10). How immense is this outpouring of love? Jesus, the only one of a kind, the only Son of God, will be God's answer to a means of reconciliation between the Creator and His incorrigible creation. Man's disobedience created the chasm between him and God; God's love and mercy is the only way it can be overcome. There can be no greater love than this. It is difficult to think of a word that sufficiently conveys the extent of this work. Stop for a few minutes and reflect on what we just read. Despite the extent of man's disobedience to God, He is setting in motion the means of reconciliation, and He is using His Son Jesus to create this means. The events foretold by the prophets are beginning to unfold.

Chapter Eight

"And it came to pass in those days, that there went out a decree from Cesar Augustus, that all the world should be taxed. (And this taxing was first made when Cyrenius was governor of Syria.) and all went to be taxed, everyone into his own city. And Joseph also went up from Galilee, out of the city of Nazareth, into Judea, unto the city of David, which is called Bethlehem; (because he was of the house and lineage of David:) to be taxed with Mary his espoused wife, being great with child. And so it was, that, while they were there, the days were accomplished that she should be delivered. And she brought forth her first born son, and wrapped him in swaddling clothes, and laid him in a manger, because there was no room for them in the inn. And there were in the same country shepherds, abiding in the field, keeping watch over their flock by night. And, lo, the Angel of the Lord came upon them, and the glory of the Lord shone round about them: and they were sore afraid. And the Angel said unto them, fear not: for, behold, I bring you good tidings of great joy, which shall be to all people. For unto you is born this day in the city of David a savior, which is Christ the Lord, and this shall be a sign unto you; ye shall find the babe wrapped in swaddling clothes lying in a manger. And suddenly there was with the Angel a multitude of the heavenly host praising God, and saying, glory to God in the highest and on earth peace, goodwill toward men" (Luke 2:1-14).

And so it came to pass, the promise of God to all mankind was fulfilled. That which could not possibly happen did happen. The young mother who had never been with a man, pregnant by the Holy Spirit, gave birth to the awaited Messiah, the Son of God. The prophecies of the coming Messiah are being revealed by the birth of Jesus Christ the son of the living God. We had talked about God opening wide the Portal to the heretofore unknown, invisible realm of eternity before the creation: Now, in the coming of His Son, God's purpose for mankind is better understood; the savior has come. He left eternity, in the presence of the heavenly Father, to come to earth to fulfill God's plan of reconciliation.

As mere human beings are we even capable of comprehending the magnitude of what is taking place by this event? In the words of the Apostle John, we realize that: "in beginning was the Word, and the Word was with God, and the Word was God. All things were made by Him, and without Him was not any thing made that was made" (John 1:1-2). The one through whom all things were created is now come down to earth and is going to place himself in the position to make a way of salvation for all of mankind. Disobedient man brought sin into the world, but it is left up to the mighty God to make a way for man to be reunited with Him. Hardly seems fair, does it? However, this is God's will that it be carried out this way. What more effective way could He demonstrate His love and mercy than by making a sacrifice of His Son? Jesus, Himself, said that He came to minister and to give His life a ransom for many. Also, that He came that the world through Him might be saved.

Likely, our first thought would be: Why must it be done this way? The best answer is that this is the Way God decreed. Another is: "Almost all things are by the law purged with blood; and without shedding of blood is no remission" said the writer of the Hebrew letter (Hebrews 9:22). Well, we know that under the old Law the people received forgiveness from sin by offering animals to be sacrificed; why not leave it like that? The answer: the people did not receive forgiveness from the sacrifice of animals. Again, the words of the writer of the Hebrew letter says: "For the law having a shadow of good things to come, and not the very image of the things, can never with those sacrifices which they offered year by year continually make the comers thereunto perfect. For then would they not have ceased to be offered? Because that the worshippers once purged should have had no more conscience of sins. But in those sacrifices there is a remembrance again made of sins every year. For it is not possible that the blood of bulls and of goats should take away sins" (Hebrews 10:1-4).

The writer of Hebrews is explaining that there was no forgiveness of sins under the old Law. He stated that the blood of animals sacrificed could not possibly take away the sins of the people. Each year, there was a repetition of the sacrifice, and this would suffice for another year when their sins again would be remembered. These sacrifices were administered by the Levitical Priests. "Wherefore when he cometh into the world, he sayeth, sacrifice and offering thou wouldest not, but a body hast thou prepared me. In burnt offerings and sacrifices for sin thou hast had no pleasure. Then said I, Lo, I come (in the volume of the book it is written of me.) to do thy will, O God. Above when he said, sacrifice and offering and burnt offerings and offering for sin thou wouldest not, neither hadst pleasure therein; Which are offered by the law; Then said he, Lo, I come to do thy will, oh God, He taketh away the first, that he may establish the second. By the which will we are sanctified through the offering of the body of Jesus Christ once for all. And every priest standeth daily ministering and offering oftentimes the same sacrifices, which can never take away sins; But this man (Christ), after He had offered one sacrifice for sins for ever, sat down on the right hand of God" (Hebrews 10:7-12). Those under the old Law who had remained faithful to God would then have their sins remitted when Jesus shed his blood. "And for this cause He (Christ) is the mediator of the New Testament, that by means of death, for the redemption of the transgressions that were under the first testament, they which are called might receive the promise of eternal inheritance" (Hebrews 9:15).

The apostle Paul wrote: "And so all Israel shall be saved: as it is written, there shall come out of Zion the deliverer, and shall turn away ungodliness from Jacob: For this is my covenant unto them, when I (Jesus) shall take away their sins" (Romans 11:26-27). The old covenant did not take away sin. Now there is a new covenant; Jesus said it was His covenant. So, Jesus is the mediator of the new covenant. "I will make a new covenant with the house of Israel and with the house of Judah" (Hebrews 8:8). "He is the mediator of a better covenant, which was established upon better promises. For if that first covenant had been faultless, then should no place have been sought for the second" (Hebrews 8:6-7). Those subjected to the Old Testament were such by way of birth, being Jews. The subjects of the New Covenant are such by a totally different means; we will cover this a bit later. At this point we will explore the reason Jesus left heaven and what that means to us as subjects of the new dispensation. Why is it necessary that Jesus must sacrifice His life?

Chapter Nine

We have learned there was no forgiveness of sins under the old Law. The next chapter of God's plan is an expression of His mercy and concern for mankind; He loves His creation and has mercy for man. He does not want man to remain in the grasp of sin. "The Lord is not slack concerning His promise, as some men count slackness; but is longsuffering to us-ward, not willing that any should perish, but that all should come to repentance" (2 Peter 3:9). Paul, writing to the Colossians: "Blotting out the hand-writing of ordinances that was against us, which was contrary to us, and took it out of the way, nailing it to His cross" (Colossians 2:14). The old law was to be declared null and void. The new covenant was to be for all mankind and would require a sacrifice; that sacrifice would be Jesus Christ, the Son of God. "And walk in love, as Christ also hath loved us, and hath given himself for us an offering and a sacrifice to God for a sweet-smelling savour" (Ephesians 5:2). The writer of the Hebrew letter said that "he (Christ) appeared to put away sin by the sacrifice of himself" and "By the which will we are sanctified through the offering of the body of Jesus Christ once for all" (Hebrews 9:26b and10:10). This was God's way. So, the Son would come from heaven to do as God had chosen. Jesus Christ as our Savior is God's marvelous gift to mankind. The birth of our Savior in Bethlehem was the most important birth to ever happen on earth.

There are events that happened for which we would like to have more knowledge. This applies to the birth of Jesus. We know Joseph and Mary were in Bethlehem due to the decree of Caesar for a tax roll of all the world (Luke 2:1). What we do not know is the date of Jesus' birth. The world has generally accepted the date of December 25 to be the time of His birth, and we usually celebrate Christmas at that time. The only fact that matters is He was born. His birth was an humble occasion; there was no room at the inn for Mary, so Jesus was born in an animal shelter of sorts and placed in a manger after being wrapped. A manger was used for the purpose of feeding cattle. There were many variations of a manger, so we have to satisfy ourselves to know that His first bed was a simple manger.

King Herod heard of the birth of Christ and requests of the wise men to find the child and bring him word so he could worship him. When the wise men, who had brought gifts to the baby, had departed, they were warned in a dream not to return to Herod with any news of the birth because Herod wanted to destroy the Christ. Then the angel of the Lord appeared to Joseph in a dream, saying: "Arise, and take the young child and his mother, and flee into Egypt, and be thou there until I bring thee word: for Herod will seek the young child to destroy him" (Matthew 2:13). They did as they were told and when so instructed they returned to Israel to the city of Nazareth.

Unfortunately, we have not been given a lot history of Jesus growing up in Nazareth. We are aware of one incident when He was twelve years old. His parents had gone to Jerusalem for Passover, and as they returned home, they missed Him, three days later they found Him in the temple sitting in the midst of the doctors and listening to and questioning them. All that heard Him were amazed at His answers and questioning.

We witness the baptism of Jesus in Luke chapter three. Following His baptism, Jesus began His ministry at approximately the age of thirty, likely in the year 31AD. In chapter four, we read of Christ being unsuccessfully tempted by Satan after His fast of forty days and forty nights, but Jesus told Satan to be gone and the devil left him. "From that time Jesus began to preach, and to say, Repent: for the kingdom of heaven is at hand" (Matthew 4:17). After healing a man with an unclean spirit, Mark tells us: "and immediately His fame spread abroad throughout all the region of Galilee" (Mark 1:28). In His short time on earth, Jesus' accomplishments are innumerable: He healed the sick, cured those with leprosy, made the blind to see and the lame to walk. He brought the dead back to life and taught of the coming Kingdom at every opportunity.

Chapter Ten

At the same time, Jesus was gathering throngs of disciples, and among those disciples He would begin selecting those who would be His Apostles. He knew when He came that His time would be short. He realized what he would endure while teaching and was aware of how his life here on earth would end. He accomplished all that He came to do. John tells us: "And many other signs truly did Jesus in the presence of His disciples, which are not written in this book: But these are written that ye might believe that Jesus is the Christ, the Son of God: and that believing, ye might have life through His name" (John 20:30-31). "And also there are many other things which Jesus did, the which, if they should be written every one, I suppose that even the world itself could not contain the books that should be written" (John 21:25). In so little time, Jesus taught so much, performed so many miracles, healed large numbers with varied maladies and inflictions that the world could not contain the history of his accomplishments. Coupled with all this, He had the time to select those of whom He wished to be teachers, to be called Apostles, and to prepare them for their ministry to the world. "And He ordained twelve, that they should be with Him, and that He might send them forth to preach" (Mark 3:14). These twelve would be witnesses of Christ and all the things He had done while here. They had received intensive training as they traveled with Jesus in order to declare to the world the story of the Messiah.

The Greek word (*apostolo*) generally means "to send with a particular purpose," so the Apostles commissioned by Christ were those who would be designated to the purpose of spreading the teachings of Jesus after they received the power of the Holy Spirit. Those chosen are Peter, Andrew, James, John, Philip, Nathaniel, Matthew, Thomas, James the Less, Simon the Zealot. Jude or Thaddeus, and Judas Iscariot. One would later be removed, and another take his place, and then later, another would be added by a miraculous event. More on this later.

When Jesus left heaven for His sojourn on earth, He knew that His Father had chosen Him to be a sacrifice for all the sins of mankind. He was fully aware of the way He would be sacrificed, when it was to take place, and all that was to follow. The time was at hand, and He was celebrating the feast of unleavened bread, the Passover feast. It would be the final time to eat with the Apostles before the crucifixion. It was at this time that He told of one who would betray him; it was also the time that he told Peter that he would deny him three times. From there, they went to the Garden of Gethsemane where Jesus prayed: "O my Father, if it be possible, let this cup pass from me: nevertheless not as I will, but as thou wilt" (Matthew 26:39). He prayed another time and then the third time petitioning the Father. Luke tells us of Christ's agony: "And being in agony He prayed more earnestly: and His sweat was as it were great drops of blood falling down to the ground" (Luke 22:44). This was the time of betrayal. "And while He yet spoke, behold a multitude, and he that was called Judas, one of the twelve, went before them, and drew near unto Jesus to kiss him. But Jesus said unto him, Judas, betrayest thou the Son of man with a kiss?" (Luke 22:47-48). Yes, a kiss and thirty pieces of silver, this was the bargain that Judas made with the chief priests to lead the mob to Him and to identify Him as the Christ. Never in all the history of mankind has treachery been purchased for so little.

"Judas then, having received a band of men and officers from the chief priests and Pharisees, cometh thither with lanterns and torches and weapons" (John 18:3). They bound Jesus just as if He were a bandit or murderer and took Him from the garden to the high priest. "And led Him away to Annas first; for he was father in law to Caiaphas, which was the high priest that same year" (John 18:13). Jesus was taken from there to Caiaphas to be examined and from there to the hall of judgment where He was to be questioned by Pontius Pilate, the Roman Procurator of Judea. Pilate questioned Jesus two times and reported to the Jews: "I find in Him no fault at all" (John 18:38b). This did not satisfy the Jews who wanted Jesus dead. They cried out for the crucifixion of Jesus, and Pilate relented, had Jesus scourged, and released him to be put to death.

Now for Jesus, there was nothing other than misery and death. He was beaten, mocked, slapped, spit upon, reviled, and was given a crown of thorns. Bearing His own cross to Golgotha, He was nailed to the cross and suffered in excruciating pain for the next six hours before He finally declared that He had done all He came to do and gave up his life to ultimately defeat Satan and sin. Christ took upon himself the sins of the world to redeem mankind, and by doing this, He was made a curse for us that we could be saved from sin. He personally carried our sins in his body on the cross so that we can be dead to sin and live for what is right. Thus, the prophecy of Isaiah is fulfilled. "He is despised and rejected of men; a man of sorrows, and acquainted with grief: and we hid as it were our faces from Him; He was despised, and we esteemed Him not. Surely He hath borne our griefs, and carried our sorrows: yet we did esteem Him stricken, smitten of God, and afflicted. But He was wounded for our transgressions, He was bruised for our iniquities: the chastisement of our peace was upon him; and with His stripes we are healed. All we like sheep have gone astray; we have turned every one to his own way; the Lord hath laid on Him the iniquity of us all" (Isaiah 53:3-6).

"By His wounds you are healed" (1 Peter 2:24, NLT). "For you know that God paid a ransom to save you from the empty life you inherited from your ancestors. And the ransom He paid was not mere gold or silver. It was the precious blood of Christ, the sinless, spotless Lamb of God. God chose Him as your ransom long before the world began, but He has now revealed Him to you in these last days" (1 Peter 1:18-20, NLT). "For He hath made Him to be sin for us, who knew no sin; that we might be made the righteousness of God in Him" (2 Corinthians 5:21). Paul to the Romans: "For all have sinned, and come short of the glory of God: Being justified freely by His grace through the redemption that is in Christ Jesus: Whom God hath set forth to be a propitiation through faith in His blood, to declare His righteousness for the remission of sins that are past, through the forebearance of God" (Romans 3:23-25). This is not only for those who are obedient in the new dispensation, but it also covered those who were obedient under the Old Law.

Later in the afternoon, the Roman soldiers proceeded to break the legs of those on the crosses, a common practice if it was necessary to hasten death, but they saw that Jesus had already died so they did not break His legs.

Chapter Eleven

After this, a man by the name of Joseph who was from Arimathaea and Nicodemus (the Jew who came to Jesus by night) received the body of Jesus. They came with linen and spices to prepare the body for burial according to Jewish tradition. "Then took they the body of Jesus, and wound it in linen clothes with the spices, as the manner of the Jews is to bury. Now in the place where He was crucified there was a garden, and in the garden a new sepulcher, wherein was never man yet laid. There laid they Jesus therefore because of the Jews' preparation day; for the sepulcher was nigh at hand" (John 19:40-42).

The Jews had accomplished their aim; Jesus was dead, but they still were not totally satisfied. Matthew tells us: "Now the next day, that followed the day of the preparation, the chief priests and Pharisees came together unto Pilate, saying, Sir, we remember that that deceiver said, while he was yet alive, After three days I will rise again. Command therefore that the sepulcher be made sure until the third day, lest his disciples come by night, and steal him away, and say unto the people, He is risen from the dead: so the last error shall be worse than the first. Pilate said unto them, Ye have a watch: go your way, make it as sure as ye can. So they went, and made the sepulcher sure, sealing the stone, and setting a watch" (Matthew 27:62-66). Evidently, they feared that Jesus would rise as He had stated He would do. Obviously, they would not admit this to Pilate, so they intimated that Jesus' followers would move the stone and take the body and claim that He had risen. They wanted Pilate to post a guard of Roman soldiers to prevent such from happening. It is a bit unclear about Pilate's answer, but it appears that he gave them permission for the Roman guard to stand watch. Whichever the case, it would make no difference because the power of the Almighty God would raise Jesus if there were ten thousand Roman soldiers and an avalanche of boulders in front of the tomb. There will be no deviation from God's plan. Ever.

Chapter Twelve

On the Sunday after the crucifixion of Jesus, the worst fears of the chief priests and Pharisees became reality; Jesus had risen just as He had said He would. They had rejoiced over the death of the Savior. They were rid of the nuisance, rid of this intruder that was upsetting all their own beliefs and desires for power. They watched the crucifixion, they witnessed His death, they saw the blood, observed the thrust of the spear into His body: it was all over with. However, they did not know what God knew. His plan was perfect, and all the misguided Jews in the land would not change that plan. Jesus had risen and would walk among men for forty days before returning to His Father.

"n the end of the sabbath as it began to dawn toward Sunday, the first day of the week, Mary Magdalene and Mary the mother of James, and Salome came to the tomb with spices to anoint Jesus. When they arrived, the stone had been rolled away, and Jesus was gone. A young man clothed in long white raiment told them He had risen and was gone, and they could look at the place He was laid (Mark 16:1-6). They were instructed to return to Galilee and inform Peter, and they would see Him there. "And she went and told them that had been with Him, as they mourned and wept. And they, when they had heard that He was alive, and had been seen of her, believed not" (Mark 16:10-11). It is understandable that there would be doubt. They had witnessed His death, were aware of His being anointed and buried in the tomb and the rock rolled in front of the tomb. However, had they believed what Jesus had told them prior to his death,

43

there would have been no doubt; it would be what they expected, and they would have been jubilant hearing the news. "Afterward He appeared unto the eleven as they sat at meat and upbraided them with their unbelief and hardness of heart, because they believed not them which had seen Him after He was risen" (Mark 16:14).

At this gathering, Jesus issued orders to the Apostles. Man has termed His instructions as the "Great Commission" and that is what it was and is: Jesus commissioning the Apostles to go and deliver the gospel news. "Go ye into all the world, and preach the gospel to every creature. He that believeth and is baptized shall be saved; but he that believeth not shall be damned" (Mark 16:15-16). Matthew penned it this way: "And Jesus came and spake unto them, saying, All power is given unto me in heaven and in earth. Go ye therefore, and teach all nations, baptizing them in the name of the Father, and of the Son, and of the Holy Spirit: Teaching them to observe all things whatsoever I have commanded you: and lo, I am with you always, even unto the end of the world" (Matthew 28:18-20). For the three years that Jesus was with them, He was teaching them and preparing them to teach all things about Himself, the coming of the Kingdom, to establish congregations of believers, of salvation from sin by the blood that was shed on the cross, and the ultimate goal of being with the Father in heaven for the infinite eternity where there are no markers of time.

Earlier in the writing, we talked of God opening the portal to an awareness of God and eternity. There is minimal commentary in this writing; we have used the word of God, as always, in the information up to this point. There is no reason to depend on the thoughts of man because they will not supplant truth. We seek for nothing other than truth. There are two final destinies for mankind. One will be glory in the presence of God, the other will find us in total devastation and an eternity of suffering. So, while we are girding ourselves to make an intelligent decision about our personal destiny, what could possibly be more flawless than having God's word and God's will be the determining factor in our choice of the course we will follow? The Psalmist wrote: "The words of the Lord are pure words: as silver tried in a furnace of earth, purified seven times" (Psalm 12:6). Isaiah said: "The words of our Lord shall stand forever" (Isaiah 40:8). There can be no question about the safe way.

We have studied a bit of the history of God's plan up to the advent of Jesus the Son of God and have learned that His Father intended Jesus to be the sacrifice for the sins of mankind. We have witnessed the brutal treatment of Jesus and His miserable suffering as He was crucified on the cross. We heard Jesus as He issued the command for the Apostles to spread the word of God to all the world. Now we will listen to their teaching and preaching and will then be able to understand why God chose His Son to be the sacrifice for sin and what that portends for all the world. Simply believe and follow the teaching of our Lord. He did so much for us, let us do for Him what He asks of us without doubt or question.

Let's remember that back in chapter six, we established the fact that there was no forgiveness of sin under the old covenant. The High Priest would go into the Holy of Holies and make blood sacrifices for the sins of the people. However, they were not forgiven but merely set aside to be remembered the following year. This would not be satisfactory in the new covenant that was forthcoming. In the new dispensation, sins will be forgiven. It would require the shedding of blood from a perfect specimen, absolutely without spot or blemish. This is why God delegated His only Son, Jesus, to be that sacrifice. He was the only one without spot or blemish. We witnessed the brutal crucifixion of Jesus; we know of His body being cared for by Joseph and Nicodemus. Now we will see Him as He prepares to ascend into heaven to be at the right hand of God. He had shown his resurrected body to the Apostles so there was no doubt about His death and resurrection, and He continued His teaching. Luke recounts: "of all that Jesus began both to do and teach, until the day in which He was taken up, after that He through the Holy Spirit had given commandments unto the Apostles whom he had chosen: To whom also Jesus shewed Himself alive after his passion by many infallible proofs, being seen of them forty days, and speaking of the things pertaining to the kingdom of God" (Acts 1:1b-3). Paul also made the statement that Jesus was seen by about five hundred brethren at once (1 Corinthians 15:6). If there was ever any doubt about the resurrection of Jesus, these witnesses would remove all doubt. While He was preparing to return, He had some last words for those who would begin teaching the story of Jesus and the means available to all mankind. They would accomplish this by enlightening mankind to the gospel of our Lord and Savior Jesus Christ and the love and mercy of our God—the most important teaching that the ears of man shall ever hear. From this teaching and through believing and obeying the commands, man can receive forgiveness of his sins and be assured of eternal life with God.

Chapter Thirteen

Jesus' final instruction to the Apostles was that they should not leave Jerusalem until they had received the promise of God. That promise was the gift of the Holy Spirit to give them power and ability to tell the story of Jesus to all the world. After Jesus had spoken these things, they witnessed Him being received in a cloud. He was going back to be with His Father.

While we are thinking about the Apostles and their future work, this is a good time to learn of the choosing of Saul to be an Apostle. He was not in the original group. In fact, he was a persecutor of Christians. In the early days of the church, the Christians were being severely persecuted, both by the Jews and the Romans. Saul was on the way to Damascus with authorization from the Sanhedrin to find Christians and take them to prison. As he made his way, suddenly, there shined round about him a light from heaven, and he heard a voice questioning him: Saul, Saul, why persecutest thou me? The Lord was revealing himself to Saul from heaven. He was struck blind but was instructed to go into Damascus, and he would be told what he must do. For three days, he was sightless, and then a Christian by the name of Ananias was sent to Saul with instructions for his conversion. Saul did as he was instructed and was baptized and regained his sight. He later become known as Paul, his name in Greek. He made the statement that he was an apostle born out of time. Christ revealed to him all he needed to know which would enable him to teach and preach the gospel of Christ. What Christ revealed to him and taught him would empower him equal to all other apostles. He became one of the most powerful teachers and writers in the church. Thus were fulfilled the words of Christ when He said: "Go thy way: for he is a chosen vessel unto me, to bear my name before the Gentiles, and kings, and the children of Israel" (Acts 9:15).[1]

The Apostles then made their way from the Mount of Olives back to Jerusalem to do as Jesus had bid them. "These all continued with one accord in prayer and supplication, with Mary the mother of Jesus, and with His brethren" (Acts 1:14). As mentioned earlier, Peter reminded them they needed to replace Judas. "Wherefore of these men which have companied with us all the time that the Lord Jesus went and out among us, beginning from the baptism of John, unto that same day that He was taken up from us, must one be ordained to be a witness with us of His resurrection" (Acts 1:21-22). Matthias was chosen by lot to be the replacement for Judas.

A significant day was ahead, it would be a momentous time that would recast the course of the world, change mankind and be a prodigious part of our thanksgiving in daily prayer. It would be celebrated daily in the lives of those who were and will be transformed by the events which took place on that day of Pentecost after Christ ascended to heaven. We are told that on that day in Jerusalem, the Apostles were gathered, and there was a sound which seemed to be a very strong wind. At that same time, there appeared to be cloven

---

[1] A good friend and sister in Christ has written an excellent work on the life of the Apostle Paul. Barbara Dowell entitled her book: The Life of The Apostle Paul. It is highly recommended reading and is available at Amazon and CobbPublishing.com

tongues of fire that sat upon each of the Apostles, and they were filled with the Holy Spirit. It was the gift; the power of which Jesus had told them.

Passover was a very important celebration for the Jews. "There were dwelling in Jerusalem Jews, devout men out of every nation under heaven" (Acts 2 first six verses partially paraphrased). It would be good if at this time you read the entire second chapter of Acts to refresh your thoughts. Luke tells us that there were dwelling at Jerusalem at that time people from every nation under heaven. He mentions about fifteen by name, so we know there were throngs of people with many different languages listening. It is quite likely that at this time there would be more Jews in Jerusalem than at any other time. The Jews were scattered all over the Roman empire, but if at all possible, they would be in Jerusalem for Pentecost.

Something, perhaps the sound we noted, drew the multitude together to witness what was taking place. As they listened to the speakers, they marveled and were amazed. They couldn't grasp that those who were speaking were all Galilaeans, yet each were hearing them in their own tongue; "we do hear them speak in our tongues the wonderful works of God" (Acts 2:11)—a miracle in itself. Some in the crowd even mocked them and accused them of being full of new wine. For those listening, they likely had no idea that they were going to be the first to hear the Apostles deliver the gospel of Jesus Christ. There is no doubt that many present at that time would be some of those who denied Jesus, did not believe that He was the Son of God, perhaps had witnessed the miracles which Jesus had performed and still found excuses to dismiss Him as the Messiah. Perhaps some of those who had cried for the crucifixion of the so-called blasphemer and asked for the release of Barabbas were now hearing the gospel and were questioning what they needed to do. We cannot know to what extent this would be certain, but Peter indicated such as he spoke.

Peter stood up among the eleven and denied the assumed drunkenness and reminded those present that they were witnessing things they should have expected from the words of the prophets. "Ye men of Israel, hear these words; Jesus of Nazareth, a man approved of God among you by miracles and wonders and signs, which God did by Him in the midst of you, as ye yourselves know: Him, being delivered by the determinate counsel and foreknowledge of God, Ye have taken, and by wicked hands have crucified and slain: Whom God hath raised up, having loosed the pains of death: because it was not possible that He should be holden of it" (Acts 2:22-24). The mighty works and wonders and the miracles Jesus performed are proof that he was the Messiah, and they could not deny this. He tells them they were the ones who delivered Jesus to the Chief Priest and Romans; neither could they deny their guilt of this action. But listen to this: you did not win, you are the losers; God raised Him from the dead, and He is now at the right hand of God. Whatever you thought you were accomplishing, you were wrong, and Jesus is the victor. "This Jesus hath God raised up, whereof we all are witnesses" (Acts 2:32). Peter continues: "Therefore let all the house of Israel know assuredly, that God hath made that same Jesus, whom ye have crucified, both Lord and Christ" (Acts 2:36). Hear this all of Israel: He is Lord, ruler, He has all authority given to Him by God, and He is the Christ, the anointed one of God, but you are the guilty party. You denied Him and crucified Him, and now you know, without doubt, that He is the Son of God, the long-awaited Messiah.

When they heard this powerful message from Peter and the others, "they were pricked in their heart, and said unto Peter and to the rest of the Apostles, Men and brethren, what shall we do? Then Peter said unto them, Repent and be baptized, every one of you, in the name of Jesus Christ for the remission of sins, and ye shall receive the gift of the Holy Spirit" (Acts 2:37-38). We do not know how long Peter and the others taught. The text states "and with many other words did he testify and exhort, saying; save yourselves from this untoward generation" (Acts 2:40). After listening and hearing those words, "Then they that gladly received His word were baptized: and the same day there were added unto them about three thousand souls" (Acts 2:41). And on that day, the Kingdom of the Lord was established.

Jesus had said: "on this rock I will build my church" (Matthew 16:18). What was He saying with this statement? When Jesus asked His disciples what people were saying about who He was, there were several different answers. Peter said: "Thou art the Christ, the Son of the living God. And Jesus answered and said unto him, Blessed art thou, Simon Barjona: for flesh and blood hath not revealed it unto thee, but my Father which is in heaven. And I say also unto thee, That thou art Peter, and upon this rock I will build my church, and the gates of hell shall not prevail against it" (Matthew 16:13-18). It is important that we understand what Jesus was saying at this time. His church would not be built on a stone (Greek PETROS, masculine gender). Christ referred to Peter as petros, and he would be dedicated and firm

51

in his preaching the gospel. The rock which Christ will build His church is a ledge of rock (Greek PETRA, feminine gender) and that would be the fact that Jesus Christ is the Son of God and the foundation for the church soon to be built. This was fulfilled on the Pentecost of which we have just been considering. Jesus' church was established; it is His spiritual Kingdom on earth.

Jesus did not name His church. His church is composed of those who have been called out of the world and into the body of Christ: as noted above those who believed and were baptized were added to the church. Because there is only one church, it did not need a name, just *Christ's* church, showing ownership. "Know ye not, that so many of us as were baptized into Jesus Christ were baptized into His death? Therefore we are buried with Him by baptism into death; that like as Christ was raised up from the dead by the glory of the Father, even so we also should walk in newness of life. For if we have been planted together in the likeness of His death, we shall be also in the likeness of His resurrection" (Romans 6:3-5). Those who did as Peter instructed became Christians on that day. They believed, turned away from their past life, and were baptized; that is how they became Christians. What created Christians on that day is the same actions that makes Christians two thousand years later: nothing has changed.

Perhaps some could ask "what is so monumental about all this; why should I be impressed with something that took place so long ago?" What does a church or a spiritual kingdom have to do with me? We briefly talked about the answer to such as that a bit earlier. The answer is destiny. For all that makes up our life on earth, all the great experiences, the wonderful temporal blessings we have enjoyed, our work, our family, our hobbies and whatever else it is that so fascinates us in our time here; when this physical life is completed, when all these fascinations fade into obscurity there is nothing then to look forward to other than an awareness of the path we have taken in life which will determine our destiny, the future. Remember what Jesus said to the Apostles: "Go ye into all the world, and preach the gospel to every creature. He that believeth and is baptized shall be saved; but he that believeth not shall be damned." The baptized believers will be saved; all others will be eternally condemned. *Is that all there is, Jesus?* 'Yes, those are the two choices from which you can pick. You exercise your free will in making the choice; I do not force either on anybody,' Jesus would tell you. Now, how important is it to you to determine your pathway? The truth is, whether we realize it or not, we are making this decision daily by the life we live. Jesus sacrificed His life so we could be freed from sin. Salvation is a gift if we choose to accept it. There will be a time when we are judged for what our life has been, and the verdict of that judgment will be eternal life or eternal suffering. The writer of the Hebrew letter stated: "It is appointed unto man once to die, but after this the judgment" (Hebrews 9:27). We might ask the question, To whom does this apply? How does the word of God answer that question? "For it is written, As I live, saith the Lord, every knee shall bow to me, and every tongue shall confess to God. So then every one of us shall give account of himself to God" (Romans 14:11-12). The Apostle John warned that we should not let this event surprise us. "Marvel not at this: for the hour is coming, in the which all that are in the graves shall hear His voice, and shall come forth; they that have done good, unto

53

the resurrection of life; and they that have done evil, unto the resurrection of damnation" (John 5:28-29).

Life is not a game; it is deadly serious. This is why the church, the kingdom is important to you. The day the church had its beginning was one of the greatest and most important days ever. The church, the body of Christ, His kingdom is the only place wherein one can be reconciled with God. It is the only entity that God will save; no other institution can offer reconciliation, salvation, and eternity with God in heaven. These are not the words of the writer, it is what the Bible states. In modern times, there are many hundreds of churches with hundreds of different names. Is this satisfactory with God? The writer cannot answer for God; He will let folks know if it was pleasing to Him. However, if the Bible states specifically how one is to receive forgiveness of sin, is there any intelligent reason to deviate from His instructions? We wouldn't argue with that, would we?

Hear Paul again: "Now I beseech you brethren by the name of our Lord Jesus Christ, that ye all speak the same thing, and that there be no divisions among you, but that ye be perfectly joined together in the same mind and in the same judgment" (1 Corinthians 1:10). Jesus prayed: "Neither pray I for these alone, but for them also which shall believe on me through their word; That they all may be one, as thou, Father, art in me, and I in thee, that they also be one in us; that the world may believe that thou hast sent me. And the glory which thou gavest me I have given them; that they may be one, even as we are one" (John 17:20-22). Again, the words of the Apostle Paul: "There is one body, and one Spirit, even as ye are called in one hope of your calling; one Lord, one faith, one baptism, one God and Father of all who

54

is above all, and through all, and in you all" (Ephesians 4:4-6). There can be no doubt in one's mind about God's wishes, He wanted unity and not division. It is the responsibility of each and every one of us to familiarize ourselves with God's teaching, His instructions, and abide by them if we wish salvation. Let's be honest with ourselves; if God wants us to be united, not divided, is it reasonable. Does it show intelligence to ignore Him and follow teaching that is not in the Bible? We need to ponder this question and decide who is right, God, or us, or others? Well, that was easy, wasn't it? Since we are discussing right and wrong, let us continue to study a bit more about this in the next chapter.

Chapter Fourteen

When the Jews on the Pentecost day mentioned earlier asked the question, "Men and brethren what must we do?" Peter told them what to do in order to be forgiven of sin and be added to the church. When they did this, they became children of God, they were added to Christ's body, His church. We remember that the teachers were guided by the Holy Spirit. It is impossible that they could be mistaken in their answer. At that point, those questioning were penitent believers, and by asking the question, they confessed that belief. To follow up with that, Peter told them what to do to complete their forgiveness. They were to be baptized in the name of Jesus Christ, and their sins would be remitted, and they would be added to Christ's church. They didn't join anything. It is not possible to join the Lord's church: He adds you. If that is the way it was done almost two thousand years ago, would it not be the same today? Has anything in God's word changed? Did God change His mind and draw up a new plan? Are the thoughts and creeds man has devised better than the way God chooses for us? "No" to all these questions, but the Holy-Spirit-directed teachers knew problems would arise. We can take a minute and consider a couple of scriptures that prove this.

Paul writing to the church in Galatia: "I marvel that ye are so soon removed from him that called you into the grace of Christ, unto another gospel: which is not another; but there be some that trouble you, and would pervert the gospel of Christ. But though we, or an angel from heaven, preach any other gospel unto you than that which we have preached unto you, let him be accursed. As we said before, so say I now again, If any man preach any other gospel unto you than that ye have received, let him be accursed" (Galatians 1:6-9). Paul to Timothy: "Now the Spirit speaketh expressly, that in the latter times some shall depart from the faith, giving heed to seducing spirits, and doctrines of devils: Speaking lies in hypocrisy; having their conscience seared with a hot iron; Forbidding to marry, and commanding to abstain from meats, which God hath created to be received with thanksgiving of them which believe and know the truth" (1 Timothy 4:1-3). To the Corinthians: "But I fear, lest by any means, as the serpent beguiled Eve through his subtilty, so your minds should be corrupted from the simplicity of the gospel" (2 Corinthians 11:3). "Wherefore let him that thinketh he standeth take heed lest he fall" (1 Corinthians 10:12). "Preach the word of God. Be prepared, whether the time is favorable or not. Patiently correct, rebuke, and encourage your people with good teaching. For the time is coming when people will no longer listen to sound and wholesome teaching. They will follow their own desires and will look for teachers who will tell them whatever their itching ears want to hear. They will reject the truth and chase after myths" (2 Timothy 4:2-4, NLT). Just a little more from the writer of the Hebrew letter, and we will move on. "Take heed, brethren, lest there be in any of you an evil heart of unbelief, in departing from the living God" (Hebrews 3:12).

Now let's take a break and reason with ourselves. If there were not false teachers and false doctrines which will condemn us to perdition, would God's word needlessly warn us about such? Certainly not. If it were not possible for people to fall away from the faith and be lost, would there be any reason for the caution? Again, certainly not, but we know from what we have read: it is possible to be lost.

On Pentecost after Jesus' ascension, many Jews believed in Jesus as the Son of God. They were penitent, sorry for what they had done, asked how they could receive forgiveness, they confessed that belief and were then baptized. As we stated previously, these are the same requirements today to be saved from our sins. Those who wished to know what they needed to do to be forgiven were just as the Ephesians which Paul wrote about: "In those days (before conversion) you were living apart from Christ. You were excluded from citizenship among the people of Israel, and you did not know the covenant promises God had made to them. You lived in this world without God and without hope. But now you have been united with Christ Jesus. Once you were far away from God, but now you have been brought near to Him through the blood of Christ" (Ephesians 2:12-13, NLT). So what changed these people? Obedience. That and that alone: they did as the Lord wished them to do.

They believed, they had faith, the teaching of the Apostles had convinced them of their sin, they were convicted and sought forgiveness. We know from the Roman letter that faith comes from hearing the word of God being taught (Romans 10:17). The evidence of faith and confessing belief is shown in their question: what shall we do? "For with the heart man believeth unto righteousness: and with the mouth confession is made unto salvation" (Romans 10:10). They were instructed to be baptized for the remission of sin, which they did (Act 2:41). The power of God's word at work. They heard the gospel of Christ and obeyed its mandate and on that day became Christians. Paul summed up the

58

meaning of the gospel when he wrote to the Corinthians: "Moreover, brethren, I declare unto you the gospel which I preached unto you, which also ye have received and wherein ye stand; by which also ye are saved, if ye keep in memory what I have preached unto you, unless ye have believed in vain. For I delivered unto you first of all that which I also received, how that Christ died for our sins according to the scriptures; and that He was buried, and that He rose again the third day according to the scriptures" (1 Corinthians 15:1-4). It's as simple as that: believe, repent, confess, and be baptized and you are a Christian, a child of God, a member of the family. Could anything that we might imagine be more meaningful than that? Certainly not, we are talking about destiny. "Now therefore ye are no more strangers and foreigners, but fellowcitizens with the saints, and of the household of God" (Ephesians 2:19). Peter said: "But ye are a chosen generation, a royal priesthood, an holy nation, a peculiar people; that ye should show forth the praises of Him who hath called you out of darkness into His marvelous light" (1 Peter 2:9). Quite an endeavor isn't it?

Before baptism, we were lost sinners, living in the world without God and without hope. Now, after baptism, we are saints, a chosen generation, a royal priesthood and a holy nation. Let's take a little time and discover exactly what that all means. To the Romans Paul wrote: "Know ye not, that so many of us as were baptized into Jesus Christ were baptized into His death? Therefore we are buried with Him by baptism into death; that like as Christ was raised up from the dead by the glory of the Father, even so we also should walk in newness of life. For if we have been planted together in the likeness of His death, we shall be also in the likeness of his resurrection: Knowing this, that our old man is crucified with Him, that the body of sin might be destroyed, that henceforth we should not serve sin" (Romans 6:3-6). The old man was put to death, as Christ was, he is resurrected as a new man to walk in newness of life, as Christ did. "Therefore if any man be in Christ, he is a new creature: old things are passed away; behold, all thing are become new" (2 Corinthians 5:17). This means that when we are baptized into Christ for the remission of our sins there is no past. It is all forgiven, and we begin with a new slate. What a beautiful blessing that is: to be relieved of the burden of sin that can become so heavy it is unbearable. This became a reality when Christ took upon himself the entirety of the sins of the world and took them to the cross with Him. A new pathway to reconciliation with God was created at that time. Prior to His death, believers labored under heavy Levitical rules. They were constantly adhering to feasts and sacrifices, and there was no forgiveness of sin. Paul said those burdens under the old law were lifted; they were blotted out because they were contrary to us and were nailed to the cross (Colossians 2:14). Now we have redemption through Christ's blood, the forgiveness of sins (Colossians 1:14).

So, we ask again: what is so important about all this? The answer is still as it was earlier; we are talking about destiny, our final abode, and destiny is not predetermined. As long as we are alive in this physical life, we have the privilege of determining what our destiny will be. Our final abode will either be with the saved in heaven in the presence of the Lord, or if that is not what we want, we can know that our final abode will be with the condemned, the unbelievers in suffering forever. It is a decision we must make, or one that will be made for us. We have seen from the word of God that Jesus gave His life so we could live. That is the greatest gift ever from our Father in heaven. Let us spend some time to consider these thoughts, after all, our lives depend on what we choose to do with Jesus. Our lives, while we are living on earth, will be determined by what we do with Jesus: our lives in eternity will be determined by what we have done with Jesus.

Chapter Fifteen

There can be no question about the truth that Jesus giving His life as a sacrifice for our sins is the greatest gift ever. However, we must remember that a gift doesn't become a gift until it is accepted as such. Prior to being accepted, it is just an offering. It must be taken willingly, and then it becomes a gift. If we choose to accept this gift, we do so by following God's eternal plan. Paul wrote to the church in Ephesus: "For by grace are ye saved through faith; and that not of yourselves: it is the gift of God; Not of works, lest any man should boast" (Ephesians 2:8-9). Man did not bring this gift about; it is God's doing, but Jesus said that all this could be accepted only through Him. He said: "I am the way, the truth, and the life: no man cometh unto the Father, but by Me" (John 14:6). This leaves no doubt; the gift is given to those who accept the terms that Jesus set forth. Those terms were simple as we have already seen. Hearing the gospel, believing that Jesus is the Son of God, desiring to turn away from the old life to the new, and being baptized. That is how we come to Jesus, accept the gift, and our sins are forgiven. This is God's way and any other way is invalid and will not provide forgiveness and salvation. Jesus said: "Not every one that sayeth unto me, Lord, Lord, shall enter into the kingdom of heaven; but he that doeth the will of my Father which is in heaven" (Matthew 7:21). "Happy are those who keep His law and look for Him with all their heart" (Psalm 119:2, NLT). John wrote: "Hereby we do know that we know Him, if we keep His commandments" (1 John 2:3). This is as simple and easy as it gets. It is so easy to do as God wishes and become a Christian. It is unfortunate that through the years man has introduced many differing doctrines contrary to the simplicity of God's way. This is not sanctioned by the Lord; therefore, we must question: is teaching and practicing doctrines that are not in keeping with what the Bible teaches, a safe thing to do? We have neither the authority nor the wisdom to judge what others choose to do, but we can safely say that to deviate from Bible teaching is flirting with an end result to our time on earth that will be totally unsatisfactory.

Jesus does not condone any sort of changes to the word. He told John: "I am telling everyone who hears the words that are written in this book: if anyone adds anything to what is written in this book, God will add to him the kinds of trouble that this book tells about. If anyone takes away any part of this book that tells what is to happen in the future, God will take away his part from the tree of life and from the Holy City, which are told about in this book" (Revelation 22:18-19 NLV). This is sufficient for us to understand the necessity of doing God's will. If we are depending on God to bring us into eternal life in heaven, then does it not make sense to depend on His words in the Bible to be our guide? I was certain that we would agree on this because we are not talking about assuming or guessing, there is no reason for those. All teaching is very plain and easy to understand. "All scripture is given by inspiration of God, and is profitable for doctrine, for reproof, for correction, for instruction in righteousness, that the man of God may be perfect, thoroughly furnished unto all good works" (2 Timothy 3:16-17). What could be more dependable for our safety than God's word?

When we have the Bible we do not need to depend on the doctrines or teaching of man.

A couple of thoughts from Jesus, and then we will move on. "Beware of false prophets, which come to you in sheep's clothing but inwardly they are ravening wolves" (Matthew 7:15). And: "In vain do they worship me, teaching for doctrines the commandments of men" (Matthew 15:9). Let me ask the question again, if there was no danger of false teachers, why would we be warned concerning them? How do we know they are false teachers? That is very easy to determine; if it is different from the Bible teaching, it is wrong. These facts are easy to understand; let them be your guide.

Let's go on to some thoughts about the wonderful blessings that are enjoyed by the child of God. We stated previously while we are living on earth the quality of our life is dependent upon what we do with Jesus. More importantly, our lives in eternity will depend on what we do with Jesus while still on earth.

All of mankind are recipients of God's blessings. There are multitudes of people who do not even believe in God who benefit from His blessings. They may deny His existence, but they certainly do not turn down His bounty. These temporal blessings go out to all of mankind. We have the earth that God created which provides the necessities of life for all, produces energy that turns the wheels of progress. We have the sun, moon, the stars, the lakes and rivers and oceans, all of which God gave us to supply our needs, we have our families which is a wonderful blessing. We are provided with the means of supplying the needs of our family. Jesus said that He makes His sun to rise on the evil and on the good, and sendeth rain on the just and unjust; so, there are physical blessings the entire world is entitled to use and enjoy. More than this, there are spiritual blessings that God reserves for those of His family, the members of the kingdom, the church. "Blessed be the God and Father of our Lord Jesus Christ, who hath blessed us with all spiritual blessings in heavenly places in Christ" (Ephesians 1:3). The outpouring of these blessings begins the moment we become a part of God's family, when we are baptized into Christ.

At this point we should take a few minutes and enumerate some of the blessings which are a part of each Christians life. It would be an impossibility to name all the great privileges, benefits, blessings, that God provides for us, but let's look at a few.

From the moment of being baptized, we have a heavenly Father, God, and the indwelling of the Holy Spirit—which would be enough, but it is just the beginning! Paul wrote to the Romans: "Therefore being justified by faith, we have peace with God through our Lord Jesus Christ: By whom also we have access by faith into this grace wherein we stand, and rejoice in hope of the glory of God" (Romans 5:1-2). We are reconciled to God and are at peace. Paul to the Philippians: "Do not worry. Learn to pray about everything. Give thanks to God as you ask Him for what you need. The peace of God is much greater than the human mind can understand. This peace will keep your hearts and minds through Christ Jesus" (Philippians 4:6-7, NLT). The last night Jesus was with the Apostles, He told them of His coming suffering, but told them that in Him they would have peace (John 16:33). How comforting it is to the child of God to be aware of His care, His mercy; that whatever happens in the world around us, we can still be at peace with our Lord in our life. Jesus also said: "Peace I leave with you, my peace I give unto you: not as the world giveth, give I unto you. Let not your heart be troubled, neither let it be afraid" (John 14:27). The serenity, the tranquility which washes over our lives when we are one with Christ, knowing that we have that presence within us makes our lives calm and reassured of God's love and care. He has made to His children precious promises that are greater than great according to Peter. We can share His divine nature, His dwelling in us and we in Him, thereby overcoming the corruption of the world we live in, supplanting human weakness with strength from Him. He will give us everything we need to live a good life (2 Peter 1:3-4). There is much more than this though: to those who are faithful to the end will be given a crown of life (Revelation 2:10). Paul told the Corinthians: "But as it is written, Eye hath not seen, nor ear heard, Neither have entered into the heart of man, the things which God hath prepared for them that love Him" (1 Corinthians 2:9). Mere man is incapable of comprehending all that God has in store for His family. We gain many hints in His word, but we cannot fully understand. We must accept this in faith and know that He has these wonderful things prepared for us.

What could possibly be of more cheer and comfort to the Christian than the promise of Jesus: "Don't let your hearts be troubled. Trust in God, and trust also in me. There is more than enough room in my Father's home. If this were not so, would I have told you that I am going to prepare a place for you? When everything is ready, I will come and get you, so that you will always be with me where I am" (John 14:1-3,

NLT). This is the ultimate exceeding great and precious promise. When He comes again and the saved and unsaved are separated; God's family will be gathered in heaven to live forever where none of the earthly woes will ever be granted entry. We will praise and glorify the God whose word guided us to this magnificent place where there will be no night, no sorrow, no tears. This will be the result of a life dedicated to being a faithful Christian. However, this will only be revealed at the end of time on earth. There are resplendent blessings which we will enjoy while here on earth, waiting for the wonderful habitation in heaven. Let's explore some of these blessings which will make our life more satisfactory and meaningful as we take our journey through life.

Chapter Sixteen

If eternal life with God is all there could possibly be, all we could hope for as a Christian, it would be worth more than everything which we might achieve in our life here. There is nothing in the entire world which we might accomplish or a desire we might strive to achieve that is as important as the blessings we have just discussed. We live in a corrupt, morally bankrupt world; but those in the Lord do not have to be affected by this. He has promised us peace. However, it does not end there, the blessings continue to unfold before our eyes when we are a member of God's family.

The Apostle Paul wrote to the Galatians: "But the fruit of the Spirit is love, joy, peace, longsuffering, gentleness, faith, meekness, temperance" (Galatians 5:22-23). As Christians, the Holy Spirit dwells with us and is our guide; He will lead us in becoming one with Christ and continuous growth in this fruit of the Spirit. This Holy Spirit dwells within us as a gift from God. Paul told the Ephesians to be filled with the Spirit (Ephesians 5:18); only when we are one with that Spirit do we enjoy those fruits that elevate our lives to the level we hope for.

We gave thought to the peace we can have in our lives so we will consider another of the fruit of the Spirit. John wrote: "Beloved, let us love one another: for love is of God; and every one loveth is born of God and knoweth God. He that loveth not knoweth not God: for God is love" (1 John 4:7-8). Our first introduction to unconditional love is when we realize that God loved mankind and because of that love gave His Son to be the sacrifice, the propitiation for our sins.

No greater love than this exists. We as members of His kingdom must evince this same degree of love. "Beloved, if God so loved us, we ought to love one another. No man hath seen God at any time. If we love one another, God dwelleth in us, and His love is perfected in us. Hereby know we that we dwell in Him, and He in us, because He hath given us of His Spirit" (1 John 4:11-13). Nothing can be more meaningful to us than to realize that God's spirit of love dwells within us, and we bestow this love to our fellowman. Not only does this contribute to the worth of our own lives, but it is something we must do if we are to remain in fellowship with God. "If any man say, I love God, and hateth his brother, he is a liar: for he that loveth not his brother whom he hath seen, how can he love God whom he hath not seen? And this commandment have we from Him, That he who loveth God love his brother also" (1 John 4:20-21). It is truly unfortunate that all the world does not embrace this concept. What a wonderful place this would be: no wars, no divisions, no hatred, no defying God's will and word. All the effort and energy that goes to feed these could be directed at making the world a bastion for leading people to desire salvation through Jesus Christ. Jesus said "I give you a new law. You are to love each other. You must love each other as I have loved you. If you love each other, All men will know you are my followers" (John 13:34-35, NLT). Jesus said that we should love our neighbor the same way we love ourselves (Matthew 22:39). Paul to the Thessalonians: "And the Lord make you to increase and abound in love one toward another, and toward all men, even as we do toward you" (1 Thessalonians 3:12). Can there be any doubt about the efficacy of true love?

How could one who is a child of God not be filled with Joy? There is the assurance that one who is in the kingdom of Christ here on earth and remains faithful will dwell forever in the presence of God. The result of teaching the gospel brings the penitent to this assurance. Jesus said: "If ye keep my commandments, ye shall abide in my love; even as I have kept my Father's commandments, and abide in His love. These things I have spoken unto you, that my joy might remain in you, and that your joy may be full" (John 15:10-11). This is the key to everlasting life in eternity. Keeping the commandments of the Lord. Abide in the love of the Lord, be obedient to Jesus as He is to His Father, and our joy will be abundant. Jesus was leading His disciples to an understanding that He was going away. He said to them: "And ye now therefore have sorrow; but I will see you again, and your heart shall rejoice, and your joy no man taketh from you" (John:16:22). Indeed they did see him again, He met with them, and they watched as He arose on His return trip to be with His Father. However, there is a meaningful promise that far surpasses this: those faithful will see Him again in eternity.

When we take some time to consider the survey of history in the pursuit of greater knowledge, as we have been doing, it all comes down to deciding on our future. An eternity with God or an eternity of suffering. Jesus endured the death on a cross, but it was because he knew the joy that lay ahead. He paid the price for sin that man could be saved and was going back to heaven with His Father (Hebrews 12:2). Then, the words of Paul: "For what is our hope, or joy, or crown of rejoicing? Are not even ye in the presence of our Lord Jesus Christ at His coming?" (1 Thessalonians 2:19).

Whatever we endure, whatever it takes to remain faithful to the Lord, we do and are richly rewarded. "That the trial of your faith, being much more precious than of gold that perisheth, though it be tried with fire, might be found unto praise and honor and glory at the appearing of Jesus Christ: Whom having not seen, ye love, in whom, though now ye see Him not, yet believing, ye rejoice with joy unspeakable and full of glory. Receiving the end of your faith, even the salvation of your souls" (1 Peter 1:8). What more can be expressed than these words of God? What more will it take to compel us to answer to our Lord?

All the scriptures we have used in this writing came from God; they are not fantasies of man. "Above all, you must realize that no prophecy in scripture ever came from the prophet's own understanding, or from human initiative. No, those prophets were moved by the Holy Spirit, and they spoke from God" (2 Peter 1:20-21, NLT). The Apostle Paul to Timothy: "All scripture is given by inspiration of God, and is profitable for doctrine, for reproof, for correction, for instruction in righteousness: that the man of God may be perfect, thoroughly furnished unto all good works" (2 Timothy 3:16). These words are holy; they come from God. We can only know truth when it comes from God; we can only learn and be strengthened in faith by knowing what God says. We are not edified by what man thinks; our future is tied to the teachings of the holy word. It will teach us the truth, show us what is amiss in our lives and guide in the right way. Striving to live our lives in the manner which God desires will lead us to all the fruits of the spirit that Paul mentioned above. Is this not the way we would choose to live, to please our Maker and build our lives on the foundation that will lead us to eternal life? "The meek will He guide in judgment: and the meek will He teach His way. All the paths of the Lord are mercy and truth unto such as keep His covenant and His testimonies" (Psalm 25:9-10).

Going back to the early days of the church, we are fully aware of the persecution from the Romans, trials, problems with doctrine, tribulation from the unbelieving Jews. It wasn't easy to be a Christian. In today's world, it still isn't easy to be a Christian. We do not yet face open persecution even though there are forces at work which intend to deny us the right of assembling and worshipping God. Then and now choices must be made, we determine to serve God or ignore Him: that is our choice. When choices are made there are requirements to be met. We meet requirements by doing. There is no such thing as becoming a Christian automatically. Make your choice and act accordingly. Do as God bids or ignore him. There is a broad diversity of choices which are wrong and will not provide what we need to please God. That is what Paul wanted Timothy to fully comprehend when he explained that all scripture is from God. Each of us need to do the same. If there is a right way and a wrong way, why choose wrong that is powerless to save us? Doesn't make sense does it? At the risk of being repetitious, think about this one more time: For each of us, the result of the life we have lived will determine where we will be in everlasting eternity. There is no possibility of escaping this truth; it will be forever bliss or eternal sorrow and suffering.

Chapter Seventeen

The title of this writing came from the image of a Portal, a door, an opening, a gateway; in this case, a gateway never before revealed to man. In that period of eternity in which God was determining his plan for all of mankind, He finally was pleased and with a whisper of His breath He opened the portal in order that every human who will tread the earth could comprehend the fact of God, of eternity and eternal life. This was all in the works before He began the creation. We have surveyed a measure of history from the Bible, all of which was leading ultimately to the Lord and Savior Jesus Christ leaving the presence of His Father in the glory of heaven and coming to walk with mankind, to teach, to counsel, to heal, to prepare teachers to lead others to the new life in Christ and then salvation in the end.

So, we have viewed now the announcement of the other Portal of which we wish to direct our attention as we bring this writing to a close. Jesus told us that He was the way, the truth, and the life: no man cometh to the Father, but by me. Jesus is that other sovereign Portal which is of ultimate significance to each of us.

"Thou shalt call His name Jesus for He shall save His people from their sins." These were the words of the angel of the Lord as he counseled Joseph concerning Mary's pregnancy. Joseph had mixed emotions without a doubt. However, he listened to the angel and took Mary as his wife. Jesus the Son of God and His saving His people from their sins is the crux of God's dealing with man.

On the surface as we read about Jesus, it is just words on a page which we have read many times over, no doubt. However, when we fully grasp the deep meaning of this information, it becomes the most important contemplation and understanding that we can have in our lifetime. Yes, this is the truth: to each of the human beings that will dwell on God's earth, Jesus and His mission are more meaningful, more important than anything we will ever contemplate in all our days on earth. It is folly if we make our worldly aims be the focal point of our lives, our activities, the way in which we lead our lives. Yes, there is a wonderful world in which we dwell, full of all the beautiful creation of God: A world with multitudes of opportunities to reach for the best, the greatest, the most meaningful heights of success which we are capable of attaining. We can win the accolades and praise of our fellowman; we can be the best there is in our chosen field of endeavor. It is possible to amass fortunes and live like kings and be admired profusely for our accomplishments, but these will all one day fade into absolute insignificance and be totally meaningless as far as our future is concerned. When that time comes, the only important thing about which we shall have concern is whether we have seized the opportunity to pass through this next Portal.

God created a Portal whereby we can enter a far more significant and meaningful life. A life filled with the comfort of spiritual blessings, a life that is led and protected by our Maker. A life of fellowship with brothers and sisters who strive to do as God would have us conduct our life; the end of which will be the prize for which we desire, eternal life in heaven, and Jesus is that Portal. Let's explore this a bit.

While Jesus came to earth to do God's will, to make a means of man's reconciliation with God, He did so willingly, fully aware of the ordeal which he would endure. He despised the shame that was attached to crucifixion, but He did as the Father had instructed and bore the burden of humiliation, the striking and scourging, the crown of thorns from the Romans and Jews. He did this with joy because afterwards He would return to the Father in heaven. All of this for whom? For you, me and all who desire to live with God forever. Can we visualize all that Jesus went through in this persecution? Do we know of any of our fellow man who would do likewise? It is hard to believe it could happen. Because Jesus followed the plan of the Father, he became the way, the door, the Portal through which we may enter if that is what we choose to do. He made it known to all how to avail themselves of the Portal. In John 10:9, He said: "I am the door: by me if any man enter in, he shall be saved." When Peter was speaking shortly after the day of Pentecost, he stated: "Neither is there salvation in any other; for there is none other name under heaven given among men, whereby ye must be saved" (Acts 4:12). "And being made perfect, He (Jesus) became the author of eternal salvation unto all them that obey Him" (Hebrews 5:9). This is the key word: obey.

As we wrote previously, He said that He was the way, the truth, and the life and nobody could come to God unless they went through him (John 14:6). He has set forth the way of salvation, and one must follow, must obey those rules. They are few and simple, easy to follow, but follow we must. In His sermon on the mount, He spoke of ways that man could go. "Enter ye in at the strait gate (Portal): for wide is the gate and broad is the way, that leadeth to destruction, and many there be which go in thereat: because strait is the gate and narrow is the way, which leadeth unto life, and few there be that find it" (Matthew 7:13-14). He also said: "If any man will come after me, let him deny himself, and take up his cross, and follow me" (Matthew 16:24). It is evident from Jesus' own words that there are requirements to gain salvation. First, we know there is a right way and a wrong way; if not, would He have discussed the two gates and ways? Certainly not, He didn't waste words. He was simply dedicated to teaching the truth. Also, there will be denial involved in following Him. That means we will be willing to turn away from the detrimental things to which we are exposed, the sins of the flesh, dishonesty, cheating, etc. These are not acceptable to Him. When we became a Christian, we were changed. "You were taught, with regard to your former way of life, to put off your old self, which is being corrupted by its deceitful desires; to be made new in the attitude of your minds, and to put on the new self, created to be like God in true righteousness and holiness" (Ephesians 4:22-24, NLT). Also Paul said: "Therefore if any man be in Christ, he is a new creature: old things are passed away; behold all things are become new" (2 Corinthians 5:17). What a change in the life of the obedient believer. It matters not what our past has been; when we become a Christian, we have thrown off all the past and begin again as a new creature with different goals, different likes and a different way of conducting our life. We are not the same anymore.

Being thus cleansed we must strive diligently to rise above our old life, avoid sin, be aware of all the pitfalls in our pathway. Know that Satan's greatest joy would be seeing one of God's family falling away. Peter warned: "Be sober, be vigilant; because your adversary the devil, as a roaring lion, walketh about, seeking whom he may devour" (1 Peter 5:8). Temptation and sin are lurking about without ceasing. Satan's efforts are untiring, and we must gird ourselves with great faith, knowledge of truth and trust in God to keep us right. We are engaged in a fight, a battle between good and evil that wants our soul. Paul told Timothy: "Fight the good fight of faith, lay hold on eternal life, whereunto thou art also called, and hast professed a good profession before many witnesses" (1 Timothy 6:12). That good profession is our acknowledgment of faith in Christ and becoming a child of God through baptism and being added to the Lord's church, then participating in the work of the church.

Paul wrote to the Colossians: "Let the word of Christ dwell in you richly in all wisdom; teaching and admonishing one another in psalms, hymns and spiritual songs, singing with grace in your hearts to the Lord" (Colossians 3:16). To Timothy: "Study to show thyself approved unto God, a workman that needeth not to be ashamed, rightly diving the word of truth" (2 Timothy 2:15). These admonitions carried out will provide the strength to resist the wiles of the devil.

The fellowship with our brothers and sisters in Christ on a regular basis is a powerful faith builder and will make us strong in the work. The writer of the Hebrew letter warned: "Let us hold fast the profession of our faith without wavering; (for He is faithful that promised): And let us consider one another to provoke unto love and to good works: Not forsaking the assembling of ourselves together, as the manner of some is; but exhorting one another and so much the more, as ye see the day approaching" (Hebrews 10:23-25). If we do not hold fast, we will drift away and become weakened and eventually fall away. That is the real importance of attending worship service, to be edified in the word and grow in faith and determination to be faithful to the end. We are edified when assembled, listening to the lesson; thus we grow. We are richly blessed as we meld our voices with the others of the congregation in singing praises to the Lord. We are at one of the most holy times as we clear our minds of every hindrance and think of nothing other than the sacrifice Jesus made for us. He said as often as we partake of the communion, we are showing forth His death until He comes again. So, each Lord's day when we are gathered for worship, partaking of the Communion is vitally important to the Christian, to keep us close to the Savior and be one with Him as He suffered for us. When the church was established in AD 33, Christians celebrated this remembrance the first day of each week; it follows that we should do likewise. The same with prayer as we and others pray, we are brought close to our savior to give praise and thanks for all the wonderful blessings He brings our way in this life and the assurance of eternity in heaven. Finally, when we have contemplated just how good God is to us, and making the decision on what our honest contribution should be and we return it to Him, we have a feeling of being doubly blessed.

Just an observation, but it looks as though some folk just do not take into consideration the blessings we receive from God when thinking of their contribution. Thinking people realize that God knows exactly our circumstances so we are not fooling Him in any fashion. Two people we know of were less than honest with their contribution and paid a dear price. In the fifth chapter of Acts, we read about Ananias and his wife, Sapphira, who sold their property and gave a portion of the proceeds to the church but indicated they had given all. Peter told Ananias he had lied to God, and when Sapphira agreed with the lie, he told her she had tempted the Spirit of the Lord and both fell dead. The disciples were new Christians, they were overjoyed with the fellowship and the promises; the text says they were of one heart and of one soul and claimed nothing for themselves but had all things in common. It is unfortunate that, to some, money becomes far too important and causes erroneous thinking. As Peter reasoned with them, the money was theirs, they could do as they pleased, but in order to seem to be more than they were, they sinned. High price to pay for being stingy with God. When we sit back and truly think about the situation, we must realize that we are dealing with eternal life, heaven or perdition: it isn't Monopoly or tiddledywinks.

Let's give this some thought. Salvation comes from the love and mercy of our God. God makes a way of reconciliation, not because we are so deserving, but because He wishes for all to be saved. He loves His creation. As we already noted in 2 Peter 3:9, He does not want any to perish but that all should come to repentance. There is no amount greater than ALL; that is how many He wishes to be in heaven with Him. He knows it will not happen, but that is His desire none the less. The idea of universal salvation is not in keeping with what we read in the text. Many believe that, but it doesn't make it correct. There are far too many man-made ideas making their own plans and ignoring God's plan from which there will be no deviation. God is patient. So far, He is still waiting to see how many will believe Him and not what others wish it to be. We do not seek eternity with God by practicing what Mom and Dad, Grandma and Grandpa, a preacher not following the Bible, or our best friends believe and do. We have been warned: we shall die and after that there will be a judgment, Hebrews 9:27. The judgment that is meted out at that time will all be from the truths found in the Bible teaching. If this isn't the truth, why would it be included in God's word? So we must give up the idea that we are capable of making our own way; it just isn't possible. Just to be sure that we are correct in this thinking, let's explore it a bit more.

Chapter Eighteen

To dispel error, we must be realistic in our study of God's way. If we were drowning and we had the choice of grabbing the rope to be pulled to safety or believe our way would be better, which would we do? Pretty simple choice, isn't it? That illustrates the difference between man's ideas and God's truths. Jesus said: "Not everyone that sayeth unto me, Lord, Lord, shall enter into the kingdom of heaven; but he that doeth the will of my Father which is in heaven" (Matthew 7:21). He also said, as we noted earlier, "I am the way, the truth, and the life: no man cometh unto the Father, but by me" (John 14:6). Those are the words of the Christ who died to make salvation possible. Do we believe that His words are important? Do we think His words are truth? Where will we find truth if not in what Jesus says is truth? He said: "Ye shall know the truth and the truth shall make you free" (John 8:32). Think about this and decide for yourself what you will follow.

There are doctrines being taught that one believing in God can never be lost. Unfortunately, this is erroneous; it doesn't agree with the Bible. Paul wrote to Christians: "Wherefore let him that thinketh he standeth take heed lest fall" (1 Corinthians 10:12). If falling away from God isn't a possibility, why the warning? The Israelites fell away so many times, and people continue deserting God en masse through the years, and it is regrettable that it will continue to the detriment of those who fall away and do not return to God. "For it is impossible for those who were once enlightened, and have tasted of the heavenly gift, and were made partakers of the Holy Spirit, and have tasted the good word of God, and the powers of the world to come, If they shall fall away, to renew them again unto repentance; seeing they crucify to themselves the Son of God afresh, and put him to an open shame" (Hebrews 6:4-6). It is not an impossibility for one who has fallen away to return to God. However, if they tarry too long in sin, it is a possibility that their heart can become so hardened and uncaring that they will not return. The Hebrew writer asserted that to be in this situation would be as if we were nailing our Savior to the cross again. Nobody should choose to do that, but it is an ongoing activity, and the more prevalent moral bankruptcy becomes the more of it we will witness. Sexual wantonness, eroticism, pornography, libidinous behavior are becoming more and more prevalent, and these are the detrimental habits that draw people away from God. Paul told the Romans: "For to be carnally minded is death; but to be spiritually minded is life and peace. Because the carnal mind is enmity against God: for it is not subject to the law of God, neither indeed can be. So then they that are in the flesh cannot please God" (Romans 8:6-8). The writer of the letter to the Hebrews cautioned: "It is a fearful thing to fall into the hands of the living God" (Hebrews 10:31).

Our God is a merciful God, but to be absolutely fair to all, there must be a limitation to His mercy. With God there cannot be a double standard. Peter said: "Of a truth I perceive that God is no respecter of persons" (Acts 10:34). So, what our life is, has been, and will be, are the determining factors in whether or not we are partakers of that heavenly gift. Paul told Timothy that godliness is profitable unto all things, having promise of the life that now is, and that which is to come. (1 Timothy 4:8). Accepting God's grace and becoming a Christian produces the wonderful life while we are here, but so much more it leads to life eternal in heaven with God. This is what we have been trying to make ever so plain and easily understood in this writing. When we accept the fact that when our life is finalized here on earth and death separates us from the world, it is not the end. Life does not end; it continues forever and forever. Once we grasp that fact, it can change our lives. We have been counseled repeatedly to know this truth and to make the necessary preparations to be eternally in paradise or in condemnation and suffering. We can deny this if we choose, but it doesn't change the truth. "He that believeth on the Son hath everlasting life: and he that believeth not the Son shall not see life; but the wrath of God abideth on him" (John 3:36).

How much thought have we given to the meaning of wrath? How about anger, rage, fury, rancor, animosity? These are just a few of the words that express the feeling that God will have toward those who have shunned Him. How could our God who is love, grace, and mercy be capable of feeling wrath toward man? God is all those things and more. He is our creator, our Father, the fountain of every blessing that we have known; this we do not question. He is also the Lord that came from heaven and lived with His creation. His short time on earth was used for teaching, healing and blessing and all other miracles and finally suffered the brutal death by crucifixion, just for you and me. Why would He not have the prerogative of seeking loyalty and adherence to His will? He has every right, and those who deny Him and/or choose to disregard His will will pay a horrible and everlasting penalty. More than once in this writing, we have broached the truth of a time that lies ahead for each of us, and that is the time of judgment. That is the time that every human being that ever lived will know Jesus our Lord. There is only one reason for this book to be written, and that is to attempt to make all be aware of this time of revealing what our lives have been or have not been, and where we will go from that point. This is not fiction. This is not meant to be entertaining; it is meant to wake us up and face reality. From this time of reckoning, our future will be determined. Let's consider a few more thoughts on this subject, and we will have to declare that we have done what is in our power to enlighten our fellowman on the truths of God's teaching.

Chapter Nineteen

At the beginning, we alluded to the fact that God, through creation, had thrown open the Portal through which all things would emanate: The recognition of a supreme being the Almighty God, His creation the Universe and all that exists within, man and all that would entail, and then the outpouring of His love, His grace, and His mercy which will endure for all of eternity. His plans for mankind have been functioning flawlessly for all of time, and His every undertaking was executed according to plan. The only malfunction has been the errors of man. The result of that plan was the saving of mankind from his sins and provide a place of eternal peace, happiness, and joy. This was to be accomplished by way of the other Portal He created through His Son Jesus. It is of this final Portal that we wish to consider as our final endeavor of this writing.

There has never been a question about God's desires for His creation. As pointed out previously, He wants everyone to receive the benefit of salvation; this is the reason He made it possible. However, there is something of which each of us must give serious contemplation, if we do not it will be to our detriment. God has provided the Portal (Jesus) of which we speak, but it is up to each of us as to whether or not we choose to enter through it. Salvation and eternity in heaven are an option; it is not compulsory. The only thing which God has set up which we cannot escape is death, judgment, and the reward or penalty that follows. The writer of the Hebrew letter said it is appointed unto men once to die, but after this the judgment (Hebrews 9:27). We are familiar with death; we see it every day, and just as death is certain for each of us, so is the judgment. The Apostle Paul wrote: "Wherefore God also hath highly exalted Him (Jesus), and given Him a name which is above every name: That at the name of Jesus every knee should bow, of things in heaven, and things in earth, and things under the earth: And that every tongue should confess that Jesus Christ is Lord, to the glory of God the Father" (Philippians 2:9-11). To the Romans he added: "So then every one of us shall give account of himself to God" (Romans 14:12). From the terms, "every knee, every tongue, and every one of us," who do we suppose is left out? It is obvious, every person, every soul, of God's creation, saint or sinner will stand before the judgment seat of Christ and be judged for what our life has or has not been. Nobody is left out. Take just a moment to impress this on our mind and accept what it foretells. We must face this truth and make the necessary adjustments to ensure eternity with God.

Listen again to Paul, writing of sinners: "Being filled with all unrighteousness, fornication, wickedness, covetousness, maliciousness; full of envy, murder, debate, deceit, malignity; whisperers, backbiters, haters of God, despiteful, proud, boasters, inventors of evil things, disobedient to parents. Without understanding, covenant breakers, without natural affection, implacable, unmerciful: Who knowing the judgment of God, that they which commit such things are worthy of death, not only do the same, but have pleasure in them that do them" (Romans 1:29-32). These are typical acts of hardened sinners whose lives are inundated with evil. What about the truly good people who are hard-working, honest, but just do not take time to know Jesus and His will?

God is not a respecter of persons, all will be judged by the same judge, same judgment. John wrote: "For as the father hath life in himself, so hath He given to the Son to have life in himself; and hath given Him authority to execute judgment also, because He is the Son of man. Marvel not at this: for the hour is coming, in the which all that are in the graves shall hear His voice, and shall come forth; they that have done good unto the resurrection of life; and they that have done evil unto the resurrection of damnation" (John 5:26-29). So, we understand from this that the distinction that separates at judgment will be between good and evil. It is evident then that we must be certain of all that constitutes good.

At times, God's judgment of the Israelites was very severe, even to the point of destruction of Jerusalem and the scattering of the people. "He that despised Moses' law died without mercy under two or three witnesses: of how much sorer punishment, suppose ye, shall he be thought worthy, who hath trodden under foot the Son of God, and hath counted the blood of the covenant, wherewith He was sanctified, an unholy thing, and hath done despite unto the Spirit of Grace" (Hebrews 10:28-29). "It is a fearful thing to fall into the hands of the Lord" (vs. 31). God's love is so intense; Jesus was obedient to the Father and gave His life for us to receive salvation. If we ignorantly or willingly fail to seek eternal life after all that was given for us, then the Apostle says we can fearfully look for judgment and fiery indignation (vs. 27). There isn't an easy way of stating that fact. We believe in God, Jesus Christ, and do their bidding, or we lose. "Therefore we ought to give the more earnest heed to the things which we have heard, lest at any time we should let them slip. For if the word spoken by angels was steadfast, and every transgression and disobedience received a just recompence of reward; how shall we escape, if we neglect so great salvation; Which at the first began to be spoken by the Lord, and was confirmed to us by them that heard him" (Hebrews 2:1-2). That is the sum and substance of obtaining eternal life in heaven with our Creator. Do not let anybody or anything mislead you, saying this is all there is. When judgment is passed, we will be assigned to eternal bliss or eternal suffering, the choice is ours to make while we have time. Someday, sometime, time will run out.

Paul to the Corinthians: "Behold, I show you a mystery; We shall not all sleep, but we shall be changed. In a moment, in the twinkling of an eye, at the last trump: for the trumpet shall sound, and the dead shall be raised incorruptible, and we shall be changed. For this corruptible must put on incorruption, and this mortal must put on immortality" (1 Corinthians 15:51-52). Again, "And to you who are troubled rest with us, when the Lord Jesus shall be revealed from heaven with His mighty angels, in flaming fire taking vengeance on them that know not God, and that obey not the gospel of our Lord Jesus Christ: who shall be punished with everlasting destruction from the presence of the Lord, and from the glory of His power" (2 Thessalonians 1:7-9).

One more thought on the subject: "For the Lord himself shall descend from heaven with a shout, with the voice of the archangel, and with the trump of God: and the dead in Christ shall rise first: Then we which are alive and remain shall be caught up together with them in the clouds, to meet the Lord in the air: and so shall we ever be with the Lord" (1 Thessalonians 4:16-17). Hebrews 10:30 tells us the Lord will judge His people. It is Jesus to whom we shall answer. "Because He hath appointed a day, in the which He will judge the world in righteousness by that man whom He hath ordained, whereof He hath given assurance unto all men, in that He hath raised Him from the dead" (Acts 17:31). "When the Son of man shall come in His glory, and all the holy angels with Him, then shall He sit upon the throne of His glory: and before Him shall be gathered all nations: and He shall separate them one from another, as a shepherd divideth his sheep from the goats: and He shall set the sheep on His right hand, the goats on the left. Then shall the King say unto them on His right hand, Come, ye blessed of my Father, inherit the kingdom prepared for you from the foundation of the world" (Matthew 25:31-34). "Then shall He say unto them on the left hand, depart from me, ye cursed into everlasting fire, prepared for the devil and his angels" (Matthew 25:41). "The Son of man shall send forth His angels, and they shall gather out of His kingdom all things that offend, and them which do iniquity; And shall cast them in a furnace of fire: there shall be wailing and gnashing of teeth" (Matthew 13:41-42). Jesus said it; so it will be. "So shall it be at the end of the world: the angels shall come forth, and sever the wicked from among the just, and shall cast them into the furnace of fire: there shall be wailing and gnashing of teeth" (Matthew 13:49-50). These passages of scripture are not intended to scare one; they were written long ago to persuade people to believe. It has been covered more than a few times in this writing: there is a heaven and a hell, and when our life here has run its course, we are going to be directed to one or the other place for eternity. We must deliberate the meaning of eternity if we have not yet comprehended. Eternity is a non-ending forever. In truth, it is more than the mind of man can fully grasp. Simply put: if we are in heaven, it will be non-ending bliss; if we are in hell, it will be non-ending suffering and pain.

We have covered a lot of years so far, from creation to present time, and discussed a lot of scripture in as simple a manner as is possible. All of which has led us to know the Lord Jesus Christ as the one Portal to eternity. We have not deviated from truth, nor have we substituted any of the ideas or doctrines of man that are not in keeping with God's teaching. If the words we have used have not caused a challenge in our thinking, we must conclude then that this has been an exercise in futility. Be that as it may, it doesn't change any part of the truth. We are at the point that we are going to have to be brutally honest with ourselves about where we stand with God and the future. We can think on these things and make any necessary changes or ignore fact and realize one day that we should have dealt with it when we had the chance to make changes. The time will come when we will not have that privilege: decisions will be made for us.

If we, in good faith, are seeking truth, we must be willing to gauge our beliefs, our thoughts and practices by nothing more or less than the word of God. The Bible is an inspired book. It will take us on the right road and no other; it will lead us to the one Portal that guides us to salvation and eternal life in heaven. God's word is the only way of knowing truth. Mankind has beliefs, practices, and doctrines that are not Holy Spirit inspired. Jesus said that nobody could come to the Father except by Him. That is easy enough to understand, and if it is true (and it is), it leaves no question of the pathway we must take to eternal life in heaven. Why do we procrastinate in accepting salvation? Our future is either salvation or perdition; it seems that one should be more appealing than the other, but some fail to be concerned. However, as we have stated repeatedly, the time will come when we will wish that we had decided to act on what we knew. We chase dreams. search for the pot of gold, and desire the biggest trophy, the accolades of man, and wish for the biggest and best of everything: all of which will be meaningless and fade into nothingness eventually, and all that will be left is where we will be for all of eternity.

We can step out of the hustle and bustle, the hurly burley of the maddening world that beckons for us to follow, to get involved, join the race for top prize and return to God and accept the truth that Jesus is the only Portal through which we can enter and become a Christian, a child of God. Jesus said His yoke is easy and His burden light, He asks no more from us than that of which we are capable. He also told us that if we were faithful to the end, He would reward us with a crown of life (Revelation 2:10). Let's think of it this way: when our life is finished here on earth wouldn't it be much better and a lot more comfortable to be right than wrong?

The prophet Hosea said: "Who is wise, and he shall understand these things? Prudent, and He shall know them? For the ways of the Lord are right, and the just shall walk in them: but the transgressors shall fall therein" (Hosea 14:9). Peter wrote: "Humble yourselves therefore under the mighty hand of God, that He may exalt you in due time: Casting all your care upon Him; for He careth for you" (1 Peter 5:6-7).

I leave these thoughts in your hands: it is my prayer that the effort that has gone into this writing will be beneficial to you and my hope is that having read and considered the truths therein, that each will be moved to dedicate your life to being one of God's children and pursue a life of righteousness and be assured of having a home in heaven when you are finished on earth.

"Behold, God is my salvation: I will trust and not be afraid: for the Lord Jehovah is my strength and my song; He also is become my salvation" (Isaiah 12:2). Can we visualize the elation of Isaiah? The bondage would cease, Israel was to be restored, triumphant over Babylon.

Now there are new and better promises to be fulfilled. In this, we see the salvation of man. Isaiah said that God was his salvation, meaning God was going to overrule Babylon, and Israel would be healed. In the same manner, because Jesus was willing to sacrifice His life for us, evil will be annihilated, Satan will finally be vanquished, and the faithful who have trusted in Christ will be forever in the presence of God.

Made in the USA
Columbia, SC
10 July 2023